DECORATING
JUNKMARKET
Style

Meredith® Books
Des Moines, Iowa

Decorating JUNKMARKET Style

Editor: Vicki L. Ingham
Senior Associate Design Director: Doug Samuelson
Graphic Designers: Chris Conyers, Beth Runcie,
  Joe Wysong (Conyers Design, Inc.)
Copy Chief: Terri Fredrickson
Publishing Operations Manager: Karen Schirm
Edit and Design Production Coordinator: Mary Lee Gavin
Editorial Assistants: Kaye Chabot, Kairee Mullen
Marketing Product Managers: Aparna Pande, Isaac Petersen,
  Gina Rickert, Stephen Rogers, Brent Wiersma, Tyler Woods
Book Production Managers: Pam Kvitne, Marjorie J. Schenkelberg,
  Rick von Holdt, Mark Weaver
Contributing Copy Editor: Jane Woychick
Contributing Proofreaders: Becky Danley, Elizabeth Havey,
  Heidi Johnson
Photographer: Doug Smith
Indexer: Stephanie Reymann

Meredith® Books
Executive Director, Editorial: Gregory H. Kayko
Executive Director, Design: Matt Strelecki

Publisher and Editor in Chief: James D. Blume
Editorial Director: Linda Raglan Cunningham
Executive Director, Marketing: Jeffrey B. Myers
Executive Director, New Business Development: Todd M. Davis
Executive Director, Sales: Ken Zagor
Director, Operations: George A. Susral
Director, Production: Douglas M. Johnston
Business Director: Jim Leonard

Vice President and General Manager: Douglas J. Guendel

Meredith Publishing Group
President: Jack Griffin
Senior Vice President: Bob Mate

Meredith Corporation
Chairman and Chief Executive Officer: William T. Kerr
President and Chief Operating Officer: Stephen M. Lacy

In Memoriam: E.T. Meredith III (1933-2003)

We wish to thank:
Our wonderful families, Kerry, Taylor, and Tyson (Ki's family) and A.J. and Elizabeth (Sue's family) for their love, support, and never-ending encouragement and for allowing us the opportunity to fulfill our dreams. The JunkMarket crew who never seems to give up or give in even when the going gets really tough. Doug, our photographer, and his assistant, whose creative genius and dedication to this book never ceased to amaze us. All of the homeowners who allowed us to invade their homes, move their furniture, and basically disrupt their lives, all in the name of junk. Peter for supplying his witty mind and words when ours had run dry. Bruce Vinokour from Creative Artists Agency, Carol Sheehan, Sandy Soria, and the entire gang from Country Home® magazine, and Meredith Corporation for believing in us from the beginning and for giving us a chance. Tom, Belinda, and our many other close friends without whose support we would not be where we are today. Our vendors, suppliers, and all of the kind people we have met on the junking trails who have supplied us with good cheer and good junk over the years. And last but not least, our many loyal junkers who have attended our sales, read our columns, and have followed our story. You have inspired us to continue on our mission.

We also wish to thank the following companies for their contributions to our book: Lemmerman Construction Inc., Detail, European Decorative Painting and Design, HardArt Studios, ID Inside Design, DKore Welding, Hunt and Gather, A to Z Restaurant Supply, Olive and Company, Re-Use Center, Eucerin, and Cabinet Concepts and Interiors.

We are the original JUNKMASTERS. We met while watching our sons play hockey and soon realized we had something else in common—a passion for junk. We discovered that while others went to flea markets to find pretty antiques, we were the ones digging, scraping, and crawling on our hands and knees to find the junk no one else wanted. But we didn't see junk; we saw one-of-a-kind furniture, humorous accessories, and new uses for recycled nostalgia.

In 2000 we started JUNKMARKET, a successful retail business that sources, transforms, and sells good junk. Together we traveled the country in search of junk to take back to our workshop in Minnesota for repurposing. That workshop soon became a haven for junkers from around the United States who wanted to buy JUNKMARKET creations and also wanted to learn how to create and style with their own junk decor.

Today the JUNKMARKET hosts occasional sales that draw thousands, some coming from as far as New York and California. We are also editors-at-large and columnists for *Country Home*® magazine, we've made numerous television appearances, and we're often on speaking tours, encouraging others to transform and style junk.

JUNKMASTERS
Ki Nassauer and Sue Whitney

From the beginning we had a mission: to pursue our passion and share it with others. And that's something we'll never transform.

Sue Whitney   Ki Nassauer

{contents}

chapter 1
Casually Continental 6

• Playpen coffee table • Cafe chair log holder • Heat lamp mirror • Fireplace surround art light • Insulator vase • Music stand bedside table • Expandable ruler easel • Garden urn table • Gym weight candle platforms • Memo board cheese tray • Street lamp table • Drawer front candle tray • Dolly and window table • String holder for paper towels • Three tiered cheese grater server • Mop ringer can crusher • Automotive wheel well fruit bowl • Street sign coatrack

chapter 2
Unusually Urban 28

• Bedspring headboard • Rearview mirror candelabra • Airport bench sofa • Canvas & letter wall art • Camera tripod lamp • Window well bench • Light fixture serving piece • Milk bottling machine coffee table • Knitting bag vase • Coffeepot vase • Ice cube drawer spice rack • Elevator operator seat wall table • Tractor drag pot rack • Time card message holder • Window frame wine cabinet • Restaurant deep fryer candleholders • Trash can table • Camera lens candleholders • Scooter picture ledge • Automotive display coffee tables • Surveyors tripod lamp • Vinyl record platforms • 45 rpm record player candleholder • Restaurant door floor screen • Gas station window washer sofa table • Laundry cart desk • Conveyor belt side table • Pulley bookends • Locker basket filing cabinet • Metal stool file holder • Sink strainer desk organizer

chapter 3
Traditional Twist 50

• Wiry chandelier • Stool seat serving tray • Architectural remnant candleholder • Christmas tree stand candleholder • Level shelves • Church chair nesting tables • Drawer napkin holder • Beach umbrella lamp • Suitcase buggy side table • Embellished serving tray • Glass shade fruit bowl • Stove top serving piece • Corbel book holder • Root beer stopper napkin ties • Hose reel music holder • Light fixture canopy candleholder • Book tabletop • Ash tray candleholders • Industrial container for magazines • Shutter bed tray • Old frame shadow box • Light fixture "flourish" easel • Salt shaker vase

chapter 4
Cottage Collage 72

• Framed wall vase • Stool side table • Redesigned coffee table • Playpen cabinet • Architectural cornice • Light fixture vase • Three-tiered silver platter jewelry tray • Baby scale towel caddy • Mantel headboard • Hatbox lampshade • Industrial tool cabinet nightstand • Porcelain light fixture flower vase and candleholder • Laundry basket side table • Plant stand candleholders • Crib rail magazine rack • Bedspring candleholders • Radiator cabinet • Baby Adirondack chair table • Birdcage planter • Screen door bulletin board • Window screen/picket fence shoe shelf

chapter 5

The Fun House 96

- Roller skate vase • Punching bag stand • Pogo stick wall art • Candy dispenser display lamp
- Toy truck remote holder • Gym ball holder table • Croquet ball candleholder
- Electrical gang box sofa table • Paint striper newspaper holder • Bread box storage
- Barbicide jar pencil holder • Bowling pin/metal number magnet board
- 45 rpm record holder mail organizer • Ice cube tray colored pencil organizer
- Restaurant napkin holder frame • Grocery-store chip-clip word holder
- Store fixture clip on basket/magazine storage • Jig Saw Jr. paper towel holder
- Dartboard lazy Susan • Training wheels towel hangers • Wire rack store fixture glass holder
- Roller skate case bedside table • Gear mold headboard • Metal stool lamp • Table leg coat rack

chapter 6

Redefined Country 122

- Playpen towel rack • Shaving mirror candleholders • Refrigerator drawer storage unit
- Waxed paper bathroom storage • Toilet tank lid shelves • Cheese cutter soap dish
- Stamp holder spice holder • Electric casserole veggie holder • Potato masher recipe holder
- Wheelchair table • Lunch box herb containers • Mail box organizer • Locker basket mail drop
- Oil cloth table runner • Caster candleholders • House numbers for table setting
- Metal base with recycled slate menu board • Tool box planter • Ice skate sharpening vise dessert server
- Picket fence swinging bed • Restaurant tray side table • Double bike basket magazine holder
- Three-chair bench • Book boxes • Industrial tool cabinet blanket storage

chapter 7

Modern Mosaic 152

- Gurney table • Glass block containers • Bathroom mirror bar • Umbrella stand trash can
- Tennis racket press frames • Toilet paper holder candy dish • Rolling desk chair table
- Cafeteria silverware container candleholder • Sanitizer vegetable storage container
- Ophthalmologist cookbook holder • Diner heat lamp vase • Industrial light cover wine bottle holders
- Shuffle board cue easel • HVAC candleholder • Car top carrier coffee table
- Thermos vase • Windmill ladder CD tower • Log stools • Cabinet door wall shelf

chapter 8

Vintage Blend 176

- Store counter island • Wash tub sink • Cheese grater night light • Cheese cutter serving piece
- Window table • Gear mold room divider • Grate & ladder book shelf
- Wire milk basket newspaper holder • Vent regulator paper organizer • Ballet bar handrails
- Theater hallway lights • Car luggage carrier rack wall shelf • Architectural molding shelf
- Drying rack photo displayer • Hospital bedside table • Gas heater easel
- Tractor disc spacer candleholders • Gear mold table • Ceiling tile medicine cabinet
- Safe-deposit box storage cabinet • Scale toilet paper holder • Advertising artwork
- Paper holder towel bar • Screen door shower • Garden fencing chandelier

Casually Continental

Open the door to a new way of thinking. The splendor of old-world design and furnishings combined with stylish junk accessories forms the foundation for a look that is elegant yet inviting.

This used to be a playpen? For whom, the Addams family?

Expand the possibilities of junk by imagining what something can become rather than focusing on what it is. This beautiful coffee table adds charisma to the room. Strange but true: It was once part of a covered playpen.

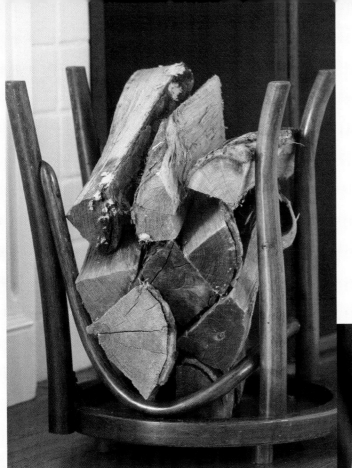

Cut the back off a tired cafe chair, flip the chair upside down, and fill it with logs. What's your investment in this project? Expect to spend about $20 and 20 minutes. Note: We tried other types of chairs and found that cafe chairs with round seats work best.

Shake up the blueprint of classic European design by displaying modified items that distinguish your own special style. For instance, an old heat lamp can be redefined as a mirror.

The weathered ceiling beams, heavy draperies, tapestry rug, and comfortable stuffed sofa set the mood for this lovely continental living room. Small junk furnishings and accessories complete the ensemble. The focus is the coffee table, hatched from an outdated playpen. A cut-down chair that holds logs, an insulator that holds flowers, and a vintage heat lamp that sports a mirror are also part of the junk team. The oil painting in the corner may or may not be valuable. While shopping flea markets, keep in mind that if you dig long enough, you can find old oils and other pieces of art that are relatively inexpensive. Give it a shot next time you're out.

9

Frame your prized artwork in an unexpected fashion—with the surround from an old coal-burning fireplace. Select one that can accommodate an incandescent light fixture. Secure the fixture with wire and plug it in to illuminate your canvas.

Our proverb stands true: A little rust equals a lot of interest in this classic metal fireplace cover.

This floral arrangement is displayed in an unlikely vessel: a large insulator. Scores of other junk finds can do the same job. What's the most important thing to look for? Make sure your selection is watertight. We've forgotten that crucial step more times than we care to admit!

Junking Tip

If you are in search of architectural junk, large, well-established flea markets and antique shows are your ticket to success. These types of markets attract dealers from around the country, offering a wide variety of merchandise. Seek out vendors who specialize in architectural salvage as well as those who import their merchandise from Europe. Kane County, Rose Bowl, Brimfield, and Round Top are markets and shows that we highly recommend.

Clean lines complement simplicity. European cottage bedrooms are pure, unadorned environments that can shelter you from the trials and tribulations of life. This bedroom is a portrait of classic European design.

Angling for the title "the junk maestro," Ki bought this music stand. She also started wearing a tuxedo with tails...

When designing a continental dreamland, adhere to fundamental principles. Choose a basic color palette, select a focal point, and accessorize minimally with key pieces that enhance the simple charm of the room. White with black accents is a no-fail choice—dramatic, graphic, and clean. An antique wrought-iron bed is the core furnishing in this room. The ivory Bohemian-style light fixture mounted on the ceiling and the mustard-color pottery add a hint of warm color to keep the palette from feeling stark. *Buona notte!*

Ahh...This gentleman is the picture of relaxation. His portrait rests comfortably on an easel made from an expandable ruler (for easel how-to, see page 14).

Can you guess the former life of this bedside table? It is a metal music stand, most likely to have been at home in a high school band room. This clear-cut repurposing requires little work: Simply position the top to a horizontal level, tighten the bolt to secure it, and give it a good cleaning.

Integrate less formal trimmings to soften an austere black and white theme. This table is fashioned from garden urns to which iron bed pieces are welded as legs. It's topped with a standard-size piece of glass that can be purchased from home accessory stores.

13

Ruler Picture Stand

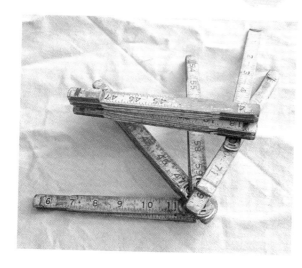

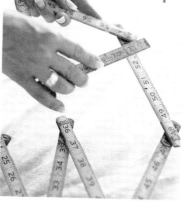

MATERIALS NEEDED

2 folding rulers

³⁄₁₆" small screws

1 small hinge
(shown ⅝" wide)

2 (2") bolts with washers

plastic tubing for spacers
(shown 1" long each)

2 wing nuts

TOOL LIST

handsaw

flathead screwdriver

drill

Frame Assembly

Step 1 Fold one ruler to make a triangle, positioning one end so it's perpendicular to the base. With a ³⁄₁₆" screw, attach this support piece to the back of the triangle base.

Step 2 From the second ruler cut a section 5" long for the easel stand. Attach a hinge to the top of this piece and attach the other half of the hinge to the back support piece.

Step 3 Very carefully, with a flathead screwdriver, pry off one section of the second ruler. This becomes the front bottom piece.

Step 4 With a drill bit that matches the 2" bolt, drill two holes through the ruler sections that form the triangle bottom. From the back, insert each bolt through the two rulers; add washers, plastic tubing spacers, and remaining ruler piece. Finish with wing nuts.

Like most of you, we adore our children and have the photos to prove it. Ready-made easels lack character, so we invented ruler easels to display pictures of our little rascals.

A pine farm table and well-worn cafe chairs mix with antiques and junk accents to serve up a room with old-world charm and appeal. *Bon appétit!*

Euriopean ambience starts with warm color tones on plaster walls. Similar hues in the furnishings and window coverings create an envelope of uninterrupted color, giving the room the feel of an ancient building in Italy. An ornate light fixture, tribal spears, and a large urn edge the continental look toward the eclectic. The junk repertoire includes a side table made from a street lamp, a memo board (the predecessor of the modern clipboard) used as a cheese server, and gym weights that support pillar candles down the center of the table. The quiet elegance of this environment invites you to sit down and enjoy some continental cuisine.

Give your arms a workout while you're decorating the table. Weights with welded-on legs make unusual candle platforms.

A memo board (something like a clipboard) makes a wonderful tray for cheese and grapes, ideal complements for well-aged red wine. Sand the wood to a smooth finish and coat with polyurethane to make it safe for serving food.

This old street lamp still shines with style. If you come across a similar piece of salvage, cut off the post and reserve it for another use. Flip the lamp upside down and have rebar welded to the post support so it can securely hold a glass top.

17

{ Sun-Drenched Solarium }

Surround yourself with your favorite junk furnishings and accessories to create a quiet, relaxing space that suits your personal style.

Every home needs a meditation space. Here the escape is the solarium. Three walls of windows invite sunlight inside and provide views that restore emotional well-being. The secondhand goods assembled from recycled junk add warmth and character. The low table, the centerpiece for tea and meditation, is constructed from a flat dolly topped by a double-thick frameless commercial window. Pick a room in your house and transform it into your own emotional restoration space. A privacy doorknob is essential—trust us!

Welcome to paradise! The showpiece of this space is a low table completely fashioned from junk. Try junking at farm sales to find dollies or other interesting farm equipment for the base. For a double-thick commercial window, check the Internet for businesses that specialize in salvaging leftovers from buildings under demolition.

The candle tray is a fun way to light up a room (see page 20 for instructions). If you can't find a cool drawer front, use any flat piece of scrap wood to make the top.

19

Drawer Candle Tray

MATERIALS NEEDED

drawer front or scrap wood

insulators

sandpaper

scrap trim

wood glue

nails

screws

spindles or dowels (for legs)

TOOL LIST

drill

jigsaw

miter box

screwdriver

Candle Tray Assembly

Step 1 Take apart the drawer.

Step 2 On the drawer front, trace around the insulators. In the center of each circle, drill a pilot hole large enough to receive a jigsaw blade. Use the jigsaw to cut along the traced circle. Sand the inside of the hole.

Step 3 Cut trim and miter the corners. Glue and nail the trim to the edges of the drawer front.

Step 4 Drill a pilot hole through each leg; attach the leg by driving a long screw through the leg into the drawer front, working from the bottom.

Step 5 Insert the insulators.

Candles can bring a touch of warmth and ambience to almost any room in your home. We have found that people are always searching for innovative holders, and this drawer front seemed a natural candidate.

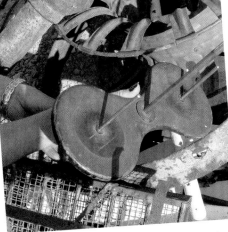

No, it's not the weapon of an ancient gladiator. It's a paper towel holder.

Subtle beauty abounds in spaces that have continental influence. Overdecorating will disturb the splendor, so add small garnishes and leave it at that!

The center of the Italian home is definitely the kitchen. This Italian-style kitchen lives up to its starring role. Stone, plaster, blue and white china, and shiny copper all contribute to the comfortable atmosphere. The junk is intentionally limited to accessories that are in keeping with the decor, so the items add an element of interest without overwhelming the room. See if you can locate the junk in this space. (It's so nice that it may go undetected.) Graters, a string holder, and a wheel well are some of the members of the junk crew that add character and function. Can you smell the marinara sauce bubbling on the stove? *Mama mia!*

Two rolls of paper towels at hand are better than one. A vintage string dispenser makes the utilitarian towels seem chic.

Lighthearted components are essential to a room even if the overall decor is reserved. Introduce junk with a sense of humor—like our wheel well fruit bowl tucked behind the copper kettle (see page 25 for a closer view) —and you will successfully transform a house into your home.

23

There is definitely a story behind this project. Who would want a mop wringer? We had no idea why, but we felt compelled to buy it. Our welder put legs on it, and when he returned, he had a big smile on his face. He threw a can in it and pulled the handle down, and just like that it became a can crusher. There you have it, folks: Everyone is a junker!

Outfit your European-country-style kitchen with a worn pine table for dining or serving. If you have a marble bust, display it on the tabletop for more old-world flavor. Offer appetizers on a three-tiered server made from cheese graters (see page 26 for instructions). Don't forget the Chianti; the bust approves.

Back entryways are good candidates for junk makeovers. People need a place to hang their coats, but there's still room for stylish junk design. Here an old street sign welded to a metal post becomes a coatrack. Holes drilled in the street signs accommodate S hooks for coats.

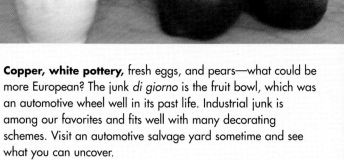

Copper, white pottery, fresh eggs, and pears—what could be more European? The junk *di giorno* is the fruit bowl, which was an automotive wheel well in its past life. Industrial junk is among our favorites and fits well with many decorating schemes. Visit an automotive salvage yard sometime and see what you can uncover.

25

Grater Shelves

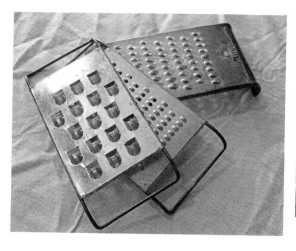

MATERIALS NEEDED

3 cheese graters (same size)
#10 threaded rod
20 nuts
4 cap nuts
acrylic plastic 1/16" thick

TOOL LIST

drill with metal bit
hacksaw
tape measure
pliers or wrench
acrylic plastic cutter or
    utility knife
straightedge

Grater Shelf Assembly

Step 1 Drill holes in the corners of the graters, leaving enough room to thread on the nuts.

Step 2 From the threaded rod, cut 4 equal pieces; these will function as the legs of the stand (shown 8").

Step 3 Insert the rods through the drilled holes, placing the nuts beneath and on top of each grater. Tighten with pliers (use cap nuts on top of the top grater).

Step 4 Cover the graters with acrylic plastic to guarantee a food-safe, easy-to-clean surface. On the acrylic plastic, measure and mark three rectangles that will fit inside the grater rims and nuts. Score with a knife or acrylic plastic cutter and straightedge. Break on a table edge.

For our project ingredients we like to use stuff that is easy to find. Cheese graters and other kitchen utensils are readily available at flea markets, junk shops, and garage sales. Remember, the key to junk style is your own inventiveness.

Unusually Urban

A hip downtown look is pulled off in style through the use of metal, hardware, and unusual industrial finds. Put it all together in a brick-lined loft to create classic urban decor.

We know it's disappointing to see a baker's rack without its buns...but just think of all the great junking possibilities.

Moderately modern is the ideal decor for loft living. Bedsprings make a see-through headboard. The platform for the mattress and box springs is a sheet of ¾-inch plywood resting on wire laboratory containers that you can find at flea markets and used medical supply stores.

Candles flicker and shine, perched on a one-of-a-kind holder, *left and below.* Attach rearview mirrors to an architectural post (or the wall) to make a distinctive candelabra (see page 32 for how-to instructions).

Make it sassy, sophisticated, and urban at the same time, *below.* Collect uncommon pieces of junk and group them together: Bea's Beauty Parlor hair-drying chair (sassy), a blond side table (urban), and a rearview mirror candle post (definitely sophisticated).

Loft spaces offer that lived-in feeling with worn hardwood floors, brick walls, and large drafty windows. Bring urban comfort to this setting with industrial junk, retro furnishings, and a gray and tan color scheme inspired by metals and wood. Are you in need of a headboard and short on cash? Look for an old bedspring at a salvage yard (or you may just find one on the side of the road) and suspend it from the ceiling with industrial chain. Junk up an urban retreat with a makeshift entertainment center crafted from a bakery bun rack or put an old aluminum suitcase on a folding rack at the foot of the bed. Make the hustle and bustle of the city melt away by creating a restful room of your own.

Mirror Candle Post

MATERIALS NEEDED

old pillar or post
scrap wood for the base and top
decorative finial
wood glue
screws
automotive rearview mirrors

TOOL LIST

saw
screwdriver
drill
tape measure
carpenter's level

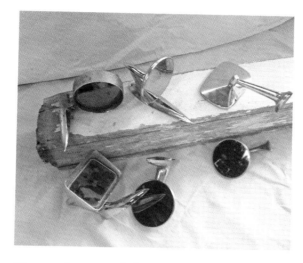

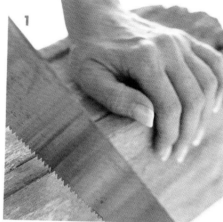

Post Assembly

Step 1 Cut the pillar to the desired height (shown 66").

Step 2 Build a base that is large and sturdy enough to support the height of the post. (The base shown is a 12" square frame with mitered corners topped by a 12"-diameter round pillar base.)

Step 3 Glue and screw the base and top to the pillar, drilling pilot holes first.

Step 4 Attach the mirrors with screws, staggering the placement of the mirrors around the post so candles will be well clear of the mirror above. Check the mirrors with a level to make sure each rests at a perfect horizontal.

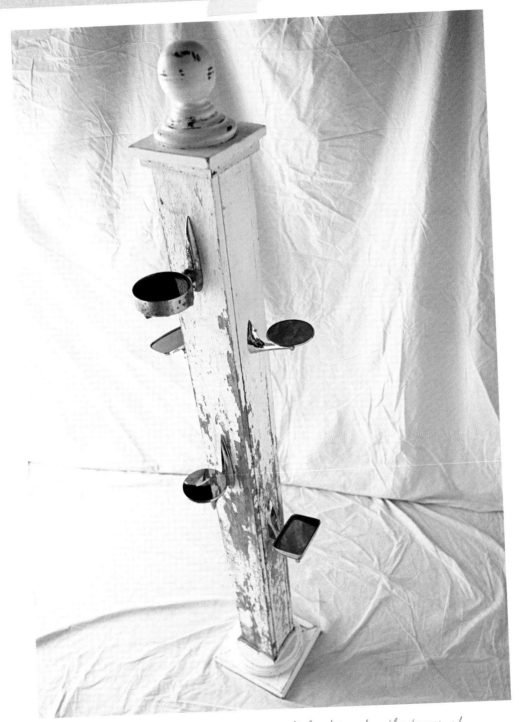

When we go to a flea market, we aren't looking for the types of things most folks deem desirable. We look for goofy things like these mirrors and challenge ourselves in the creativity department.

g

w

The junk menagerie in this room includes a coffee table made from a milk-bottling machine, a camera tripod lamp, a window well conversation bench, a knitting bag vase, weathered letters for wall art, and an airport bench sofa.

This downtown dwelling blends modern living with a mix of junk from farm to industrial. It's an avant-garde approach to decorating that delivers attitude and the look of high design without the lofty prices.

Inspire yourself by taking a junking excursion to a building re-use center, where window wells can be found for around $2.50. What a steal! We were thinking conversation bench, and after a few failed attempts, we came up with a cozy little love seat that fits perfectly into any loft living room (see page 38 for instructions to make a similar one yourself).

An architectural feature (such as a fireplace) or a great piece of art often serves as the focal point of a room. In a junk-style room, the focus is likely to be the most unusual object that grabs your attention and anchors the space—such as a coffee table (*left*) made from a milk-bottling machine. Surround your repurposed salvage with cool colors, geometric patterns, and a blend of textures to create a sleek yet inviting atmosphere. When guests arrive, your one-of-a-kind cast-off conversation pieces are sure to spawn a lively discussion. "Where do you buy your junk?"

This space is shaken, not stirred, for perfect urban flavor. Now all you have to do is kick back, relax, and enjoy your view of the city skyline. It's five o'clock; martini, anyone?

Lofts typically have high ceilings and long walls looking for artwork. Make your own graphic art by attaching a large metal signage letter to a painted canvas. You'll love the look, not to mention the money you save.

35

We've got the milk machine. Now all we need is a truckload of cookies.

Make a coffee table from sleek stainless steel and glass. What's the base of the table? It's the tank and bottle holder from a milk-bottling machine. What's on top? Mmmm...blue martinis! They go well with the nuts served in a former light fixture.

Junking Tip

To find junk that has urban appeal, check out a restaurant supply store. You'll discover a wide variety of stainless-steel pieces that will complement an urban decorating theme. Look for prep tables and bakery racks that can be easily converted for use in your home. Items that appear a little too worn for restaurant use will be less expensive than pieces that can still fulfill their intended purpose. **Happy hunting!**

A knitting bag with panache is called to stand in as a flower vase. The graphic pattern and retro colors make it a striking addition to a space with a futuristic feeling.

Groovy Bench

MATERIALS NEEDED

1×4s

wood glue

2 old shallow-depth galvanized window wells

7 (¹/₄×1¹/₂") carriage bolts

7 locking nuts

3 washers

random-length discarded mahogany and cherry wood trim

4 heavy-duty casters

TOOL LIST

router

bar clamps

drill with ⁵/₁₆" bit

socket wrench

miter saw

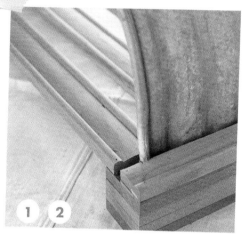

Bench Assembly

Step 1 Glue and fasten together 1×4 blocks for the base. Route out to accept the window well flanges.

Step 2 Place flange of window well into the routed area and clamp together with bar clamps. Glue and install the bottom runners for lower storage and support.

Step 3 Place top well on the bottom assembly. Drill three ⁵/₁₆" holes through the wells. Insert ¹/₄×1¹/₂" carriage bolts into the holes; fasten with locking nuts.

Step 4 Miter the return ends on the bull nosing used for the armrests and affix matching cherry casing to the top. Fasten to upper flanges with ¹/₄×1¹/₂" carriage bolts.

Step 5 Attach casters.

Note: Finished seating height is 18" to 20". Adjust dimensions as needed. Refinish wood before assembly.

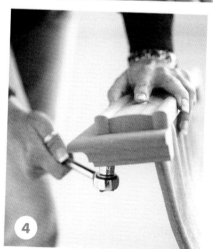

5

Building with really funky materials is what we are all about. Flip it upside down or sideways and get a view of your junk canvas from every angle. We really had to use our thinking caps for this project.

The term is no longer Dumpster diving; now it's Dumpster dining! An old trash can (well-washed, of course) is the base for this one-of-a-kind table.

No need to designate a driver for this progressive dinner: Whip up a culinary masterpiece in your kitchen and serve it up just a few steps away in the dining area. Lofts often consist of only one main living area, so spaces are defined by purpose instead of walls. Use junk to set the boundaries between areas: For instance, an island made from an industrial worktable frame and a butcher-block top *opposite* divides the kitchen from the dining space. The island does triple duty as a food preparation surface, a place for snacking, and a display table for a coffeepot filled with flowers.

An elevator operator seat mounted on the wall above waist height makes a perfect catchall for purse and keys (see page 42 for another view).

An old ice cube drawer keeps spices organized and easily accessible. To give the tray legs, we had a welder bend two pieces of rebar and weld them to each end of the tray.

Farm equipment in a hip and trendy loft? Why not? The pot rack was originally a drag pulled behind a tractor. You are more than likely to find one of these or a similar piece at a farm auction. Hire a welder to attach wall brackets for hanging and to bend the prongs so they'll hold pots and pans. For safety, hang heavy items like this on wall studs or use heavy-duty toggle bolts.

Store your wine in a cabinet crafted from an old window frame, recycled painted wood, and the base of a typewriter stand. On top, deep fat fryers from a restaurant supply store twinkle with the light of pillar candles.

Ki models the latest in junk accessories. Finding the right necklace can be such a pane!

Free yourself from decorating inhibitions and have fun with your space. If the garbage can table isn't enough fun on its own, add a time card holder on the wall for messages and a telephone table made from an elevator operator seat. It's urban decor any way you work it!

Industrial waste cans make excellent table bases—after they're well cleaned. Wash thoroughly with a bleach solution. Spray-paint the outside or simply apply a coat of polyurethane to maintain its patina. A store-bought glass round is the tabletop. For a citified dining experience, set candles in old camera lenses. Did you ever think you would be dining on a trash can by choice?

Are you an amateur photographer? Use an old lens as a candleholder and shed some light on your hobby.

Oh, the possibilities ...We'll let you decide what to keep in these tins. We, of course, use them to store our galoshes.

An old scooter makes eye-catching wall art. Look for scooters at flea markets or garage sales. If you find ones that are in rough shape, you may get a better deal. Have a welder attach wall brackets for easy hanging.

When is a door not a door? This swinging door from a restaurant stands still in a frame to serve as a floor screen. The wall-mounted magazine rack turns favorite publications into art.

Just about anything goes when you're decorating downtown digs. New upholstered furniture with clean, modern lines partners well with repurposed industrial junk, which has the same clean lines and adds the bonus element of surprise. For example, check out the pair of coffee tables. The tabletops are from an old automotive display rack, and the frames are made from new steel pipe and casters. The candleholder on display is a 45-rpm record player. Slide a restaurant worktable against the wall for a credenza, set out some munchies on serving trays made from old records, and make a tripod into a floor lamp for a totally metro look.

Serve up your munchies in record time. Locate old, thick vinyl records and mount them on metal bases made of floor flanges, steel pipe, and nipples from a hardware store.

An outdated gas station window washer makes an amazing sofa table. Steel rods welded to the top support the glass surface at the right height.

{Junk at Work}

This office has so many cool junk gadgets that you may actually have fun at work!

Ki finds the kiddie cart a big help to keep the young ones in line while shopping for junk.

Locker baskets are ideal for filing; they're also indispensable organizers for kids' rooms, the garage, and the laundry room. A metal stool flipped upside down, *right*, works well as a file holder.

This office represents the ultimate in urban industrial design. If this is the look you're after, be patient and build your office one piece of junk at a time. You'll need to do an extensive talent search to locate your entire cast of characters. The main attraction here is a retired laundry cart revamped as a desk: off with the canvas; on with the wood shelves and desk top. Brackets welded to the metal struts hold the shelves in place. An industrial bread rack filled with locker baskets surpasses any purchased file cabinet in storage potential and character. The credenza in front of the window started out as a conveyor belt; a glass top and metal rod legs welded to its frame turn it into a functional work surface. Once you have assembled the main players, start collecting junk for the minor roles: Use pulleys as bookends, build your own desk tray using sink strainers and doorstops (see page 48 for instructions), and flip a metal stool upside down to hold active files. Recruit your junk with creativity, and the production will be a box office smash!

A newly made wood box outfitted with sink strainers and doorstops acts as a home for your desk supplies.

47

Desk Accessory Tray

MATERIALS NEEDED

wood
sink strainers
glue
screws
4 flip-down door stops

TOOL LIST

jigsaw
pencil
circle stencil or compass
tape measure
drill
miter box
screwdriver

Tray Assembly

Step 1 Cut the board to hold the strainers (shown 5"×24").

Step 2 Position the strainers upside down on the board; trace around them with a pencil. Remove the strainers and draw a second circle ⅛" inside each traced circle. This is the cutout area.

Step 3 Drill a hole in the side of the inner circle to insert the jigsaw.

Step 4 Cut out the circle with a jigsaw.

Step 5 Cut trim with enough surface to attach the legs; miter the corners.

Step 6 Glue and screw trim to the board.

Step 7 Finish the wood as desired.

Step 8 Attach the doorstops with screws.

Step 9 Slip the strainers into the holes.

When designing for urban and modern spaces, we look for shiny objects. You can find sink strainers at many different junk hot spots, such as flea markets and building re-use centers. The strainers were naturals for paper clips and other small supplies. We always say, build it and they will come.

Traditional Twist

Traditional furnishings and junk accessories make perfect dance partners; coordination is the key. Enhance time-honored decor with a handful of junk adaptations and give your home a turn for the better.

Is this a traditional dining room? Yes, but look for tabletop accessories that are far from standard traditional fare—for example, a serving tray fashioned from a stool seat, with drawer pulls for handles. The tray was rendered food-safe by thorough cleaning, a bit of sanding, and a coat of polyurethane.

The essence of the Traditional Twist design concept is the use of junk to relax the feel of traditionally furnished environments. When this concept is executed well, the junk blends so that you hardly notice its presence. This dining room is a fine representation of the style. A British Colonial dining room seems conventional at first blush, but take a closer look and you will find a tabletop that's breaking all the rules. It's bursting with tag sale redos that are beautiful as well as functional. The junk transformations include a serving tray made from a discarded stool seat, a drawer turned napkin holder, a wiry chandelier, and glimmering candles set on pieces of architectural salvage. (For instructions on making your own footed drawer, see page 56.) These seemingly minor junk side dishes make a bold decorating statement and help establish a space that is both formal and funky—now that's a true revolution!

Add interest to your mantel with a display of unusual objects, *right*. The candleholder is an upside-down glass lampshade resting in an old Christmas tree stand. Look to specialty dealers at flea markets to find vintage holiday goods.

Set your buffet table with a blend of old and new, *far right*. Vintage bases support new glass hurricane globes, a stool seat acts as a serving tray, and a footed drawer displays napkins.

This elegant chandelier, *above right,* is an iron garden ornament combined with a round wooden pillar base, both found at an architectural salvage store. Have a welder add a rebar lip around the base; then join the pieces with old chain and suspend the chandelier from the ceiling.

If you're looking for a clever way to display your treasures, here's the solution. Mount levels of varying sizes on the wall with metal L brackets. Hanging them straight will be a snap.

Ki does her best to keep a level head while surrounded by so much cool junk.

Converting church chairs into nesting tables (right)—it may be our calling.

Junking Tip

When shopping a flea market or other favorite junking haunt, seek out ordinary items that you can turn into the extraordinary.

Church chairs, floor grates, and carpenter's levels are just a few examples of things that are readily available. Choose pieces that you like and believe will work together. If your project doesn't work out the way you thought, don't fret; you can always try something else.

After all, it's only junk!

The combination of two church chairs and two wooden floor grates results in distinctive nesting tables. On the larger table, a floor grate forms the top, the chair seats become stationary side extensions, and leftover lumber from the chairs is refashioned into legs. The smaller table also has a grate for a top, and the crisscross portions of the old chair legs support it. The smaller table slides underneath the larger one and rests on the chair seats.

Levels are ideal photo displayers. Thanks to their construction, they provide a natural beveled edge to hold picture frames in place.

55

Drawer Napkin Holder

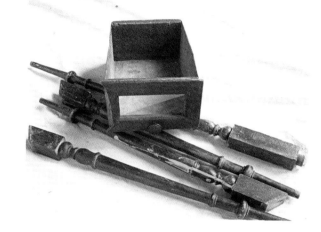

MATERIALS NEEDED

4 spindles
old drawer
4 (1¼") wood screws
wood glue

TOOL LIST

handsaw or jigsaw
drill
³⁄₃₂" drill bit
phillips head screw bit

Holder Assembly

Step 1 Saw 4 matching 1½"-long sections from spindles.

Step 2 Drill pilot holes in the bottom of the drawer and in the top of each spindle, using a ³⁄₃₂" drill bit. Attach spindles to the bottom of the drawer with 1¼" screws and glue.

Note: Knobs or small wood blocks can be used instead of spindles for feet.

We often find stray drawers while hunting for project materials.
This one is unique because of its metal sides, so without hesitation
we brought it back to the shop for a makeover.

Make a lamp base from the frame of a beach umbrella turned upside down. Run a hollow pipe down the center and fit it with lamp parts purchased from a hardware store.

After performing their traditional junk dance, Ki and Sue wait for the results.

Step inside an inviting sunroom shaped by traditional architecture and sophisticated West Indies furnishings. Notice the combination of textures, from nubby burlap to dark rattan and wood. Together these elements create a quiet place to while away the afternoon hours in high style. To soften the mood, adorn the room with a few carefully chosen junk items that enhance rather than compete with the lovely decor. A lamp fashioned from a beach umbrella wears a purchased leather lampshade chosen to complement the overall style of the space. A vintage suitcase with rich colors rests on buggy wheels to serve as a side table. A serving tray receives a facelift: fresh paint and a new bottom—woven blind material layered under glass. The traditional building blocks in this room comingle with junk to create an atmosphere of total tranquillity. Now you can settle down and finally finish *War and Peace* (or at least this week's *People*).

Old suitcases add a touch of warmth to any space. We needed a side table, so we simply placed the suitcase on top of old buggy wheels and frame. It's a straightforward idea—no tools required.

59

The unusual serving piece at the far end of the island is fabricated from an old stove top and wood slats, which form the serving surface. A coat of polyurethane keeps the rusty finish from flaking.

Welcome to a classic French Country kitchen. The painted and distressed cabinets, beamed ceiling, and furniture-style island set the stage for a traditional junk makeover. Go easy, though. A kitchen like this needs only a touch of makeup. When searching for cast-off materials to repurpose in a French Country room, choose pieces such as architectural salvage, ornate metal items, and decorative glass; these will blend nicely with the look you've already established. This kitchen gains charm and character from subtle junk touches: a fruit bowl born from the marriage of a footed iron base and a fancy glass light fixture, an old stove top acting as a serving piece, and (beside the oven) a cookbook holder made from a carved wooden corbel. In the junkers' handbook, this type of makeover is known as perfect imperfection.

Vintage electrical wire is the starting point for these unusual napkin rings. For an extra touch of fun add an old root beer stopper. Finding and using unexpected objects is one of the most exciting aspects of junking.

Available by the dozens at almost any flea market, glass ceiling-light fixtures are one of the most versatile items in the junk decor world. This fixture became a fruit bowl when we attached it to an iron base with a nut and bolt.

We used it as a fruit bowl, but it also makes a great hat.

The furnishings in this formal living room, combined with the rich color scheme and enameled woodwork, give the space a classic British look. Such a sophisticated room requires sophisticated and subtle junk. "Less is more" is the watchword when accessorizing with junk in a cultured space. Here, for example, the side table is a quick but clever addition. We started with a small table and set a worn, leather-bound book on top to create a larger surface. No need to permanently attach it; instead, cut a nonslip rug pad to size to hold the book in place. Other junk garnishes appear on the coffee table: candles placed in vintage ashtrays and magazines neatly stored in an industrial container. On the piano a candle rests on an antique light fixture canopy that holds a new glass hurricane globe. Next to the piano bench, a modified hose reel houses music books.

In junking, as in evolution, those who survive are those who adapt! Junk adapted to tasteful trimmings survives to have a second life as accessories that complement the upscale decor of this room. Style, sophistication, satisfaction— junking provides it all.

A beautiful coffee table adorned with junk adds warmth to this environment. Where's the junk? Ashtrays hold the candles, and an industrial wire basket contains magazines.

63

We had an old table base in need of a new top. Our replacement choice? The world's largest book (we also have a table made out of the world's smallest book, but it's harder to set a drink on).

Ah! There's nothing like relaxing in the tub with a good book!

Use a hose reel to hold sheet music? Yes indeed! Add some bamboo pieces cut to size and there you have it. (See page 66 for the how-to.)

Hose Reel Magazine Rack

MATERIALS NEEDED

bamboo
wooden hose reel
1" or 1¼" brads
stain marker

TOOL LIST

fine-tooth saw
tape measure
drill with ¹⁄₁₆" drill bit
tack hammer

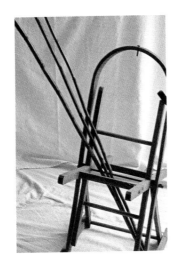

Rack Assembly

Step 1 Cut bamboo to the width of the crossbars of the hose reel. Cut enough lengths to cover two sections of crossbars.

Step 2 Working from the inner edge out, use a tack hammer and brads to secure the bamboo to the hose reel. (Predrill brad holes to avoid splitting the bamboo.)

Step 3 Finish freshly cut ends of bamboo with a stain marker.

Note: Narrow wood or dowels may be used in place of bamboo.

We found this primitive hose reel at a corner antique store. If there hadn't been a hose wrapped around it, we might not have known what it was. Its construction and color were just right for the project at hand.

[Tropical Sleeping Quarters]

Furnishings reminiscent of the Old South paired with refined junk offer a breezy, tropical getaway right in your own home. It's a breath of fresh air!

A serene white background comes to life through the incorporation of vivid tropical prints, bright accents, and a mixture of textures. These combine with traditional furnishings to create the spirit of life on a tropical plantation. An even more blissful environment can be achieved by including a few simple junkables. A bed tray is a must-have item in any bedroom retreat. Make one out of old shutters, which are easy to find and usually inexpensive (see page 70 for how-to). Broken frames are also tops on our list of junk materials. Build a shadow box behind the frame, using recycled wood for the shelves, and hang it on the wall to display family photos. Treat yourself to fresh flowers—a big bouquet in a vintage jar or a tiny sprig in a salt shaker—and use a flourish or finial from a light fixture as a picture rest. The junk details make the room a personalized haven of comfort and calm.

A broken frame can be repurposed as a shadow box, *right,* to display family photos and postcards.

A metal flourish from a light fixture, *far right,* was separated from the rest of the lamp components somewhere along the road. Now it's highlighted as an interesting picture easel.

Old shutters, *above right,* are a dime a dozen in the junking world and can be found just about anywhere. We put this set to good use as a bed tray. Breakfast in bed, anyone?

Shutter Bed Tray

MATERIALS NEEDED

wood chair
wood trim
hinged cafe shutter
1" finishing nails
wood glue
1⅝" wood screws
⅛" glass

TOOL LIST

handsaw
tape measure
miter box
hammer
screwdriver
glass cutter
gloves

Tray Assembly

Step 1 Remove chair seat, chair back, and front and back support rails. Cut chair legs to desired height (shown finished height is about 11").

Step 2 Cut trim to fit edges of shutter, mitering the corners.

Step 3 Attach trim to shutter edges with finishing nails and glue; assemble so that shutter handles face down.

Step 4 Attach shutter to chair base with screws.

Step 5 Paint or finish as desired.

Step 6 Cut two pieces of ⅛" glass to fit inside the louvered areas.

A bedroom retreat would be incomplete without breakfast in bed. To satisfy this requirement we built a bed tray to suit the mood of the room.

Cottage Collage

Enhance the cozy feel of a summer cottage with a few junk flourishes. Crisp whites and pastels serve as a backdrop for a clean look that is sometimes sweet and never fussy. Whether you have an actual cottage or a downtown apartment, this decor will create the getaway you've been seeking.

To save a table with a bad veneer top, remove the top and cut the legs down; flip the top upside down and reattach it to the legs. Use wood glue to affix the leftover pieces of legs to the rim of the table skirt. Paint the entire piece and top it with glass. If the table is a nonstandard size, have a glass cutter trim a piece of heavy glass to the right size and grind the edges for a smooth finish.

This sitting room is pretty in pastels, a classic color scheme for cottage settings. The window covering, a simple sheer panel, lets attention focus on the cornice, which is constructed from chipped-paint architectural salvage. The cabinet and the coffee table look so natural in this setting that no one would suspect they are junk creations. The cabinet was once a playpen and the table a more conventional Early American-style piece.

Build a clever cornice from a piece of old baseboard; nail decorative molding to the back of the board.

Take something that most people view as hopeless and make it something special. A playpen that has outlived its life with children can still be converted into something useful. Dismantle the playpen, reformat it, and put it all back together again. Use all the original parts and incorporate some additional salvaged materials (such as beaded board for the back) and you will end up with an original screen cabinet. Child's play!

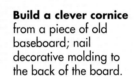

So many types of molding. Our favorite? Medium hand-tossed.

Sue emerges from the junking underworld.

Framed Vase

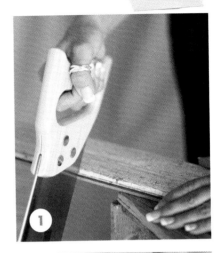

MATERIALS NEEDED

beaded board

frame (shown 8×17)

nails

bottle with a
   neck that will fit in
   the broom clip

broom clip

screws

old chain

decorative knobs
   for the wall

TOOL LIST

saw

tape measure

hammer

screwdriver

Framed Vase Assembly

Step 1 Saw the beaded board to fit into the frame opening.

Step 2 Attach the beaded board to the frame with small nails.

Step 3 Place the bottle in the broom clip and center it in the frame. Remove the bottle and mark the position.

Step 4 Attach the broom clip with screws.

Step 5 Secure the bottle in the clip.

Step 6 Attach chain to the back of the beaded board for hanging. Suspend from a decorative knob or hardware piece.

Note: If you start with a shiny new broom clip, leave it in water for a few days to rust.

A junker, like an artist, often works with a variety of media. We love combining lots of different materials to produce one project. This wall vase boasts a perfect blend of wood, glass, and metal.

Junk extras add personality
to an all-white cottage-style
bathroom. Look for mirrors in
hefty vintage frames and layer
them to supply architectural
character as well as reflected
natural light.

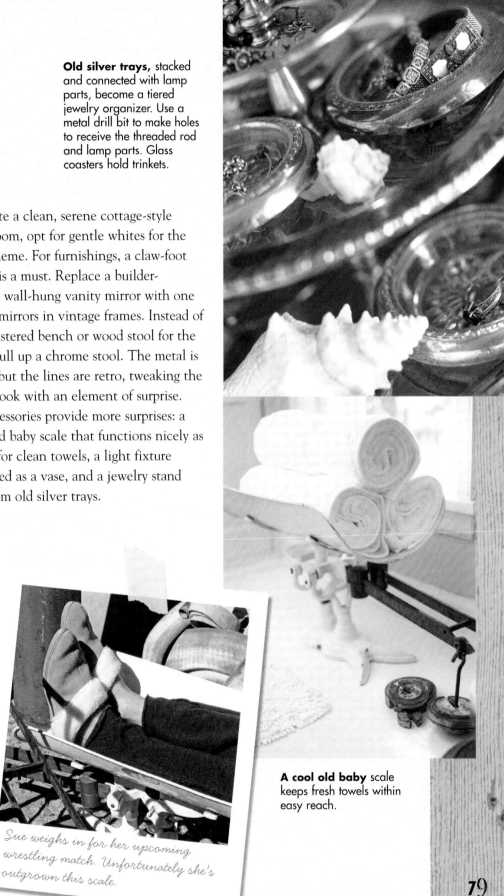

Old silver trays, stacked and connected with lamp parts, become a tiered jewelry organizer. Use a metal drill bit to make holes to receive the threaded rod and lamp parts. Glass coasters hold trinkets.

To create a clean, serene cottage-style bathroom, opt for gentle whites for the color scheme. For furnishings, a claw-foot bathtub is a must. Replace a builder-supplied, wall-hung vanity mirror with one or more mirrors in vintage frames. Instead of an upholstered bench or wood stool for the vanity, pull up a chrome stool. The metal is modern but the lines are retro, tweaking the cottage look with an element of surprise. Junk accessories provide more surprises: a recovered baby scale that functions nicely as a caddy for clean towels, a light fixture repurposed as a vase, and a jewelry stand made from old silver trays.

Sue weighs in for her upcoming wrestling match. Unfortunately she's outgrown this scale.

A cool old baby scale keeps fresh towels within easy reach.

Make a guest bedroom welcoming with pretty pastel prints and an architectural headboard that will wow your overnight company. Arrange fresh flowers to show you care.

Portray the sweeter side of cottage decor with a soft pink and green guest bedroom. This type of cottage room calls out for delicate pastel prints and vintage fabrics that warm the white backdrop. How do you begin putting a room together? Formulate a decorating scheme and choose a focal point for the space. In a bedroom the headboard is a typical focal point, and inventiveness with this component has a big impact. Discarded mantels are one avenue to distinctive design. Every time a home or an old hotel is torn down to make way for a more modern facility, mantels and other fabulous architectural pieces are left behind. Look to specialty dealers at flea markets or architectural salvage stores for a good selection of mantels. Be forewarned though: With a room this enticing, your guests may want to extend their stay.

Try something off-the-wall. A steel industrial tool cabinet may seem unattractive at first glance; have it sandblasted and powder coated in a crisp white, and before your eyes the ugly duckling will become a swan. Check the Yellow Pages for powder coaters and ask them to recommend a sandblaster. Auto body shops may also be able to direct you to the appropriate company.

Every bedroom calls for a flower vase, but why settle for the predictable? Take two porcelain light fixtures, stack one on the other, and fill with peonies. Tell your guests it's an eclectic electric vase.

Little did this hatbox suspect it would soon have a new life as a lampshade. Ah, destiny!

81

Mantel Headboard

MATERIALS NEEDED

1×8 boards
mantel
corrugated metal
paint
screws
1×2 boards

TOOL LIST

saw
tape measure
tin snips or jigsaw
    with a blade for metal
drill
paintbrush
sandpaper or
    palm sander
screwdriver

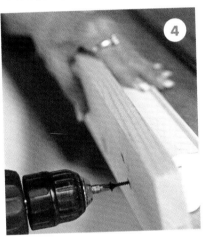

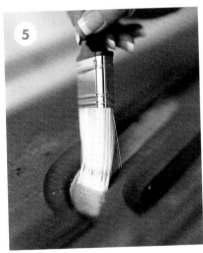

Headboard Assembly

Step 1 Cut two 1×8 boards to the desired height of the headboard (shown 61" finished height; we added 12" to the original mantel). Attach with screws to back of mantel as a base. Cut additional lengths of 1×8s and attach them to the base as pedestals for the molded and trimmed sides.

Step 2 Cut the metal to fit opening; add a 2" allowance for attaching to the back of the mantel. Predrill holes in the metal.

Step 3 Build up the sides, if needed, using 1×2 boards (we made ours 1" deeper).

Step 4 Add a mantel shelf if necessary (shown 5" deep).

Step 5 Paint. After the paint dries completely, run the sander lightly over edges and corners to distress the finish.

Step 6 Attach the metal to the back of the mantel with screws.

Note: Pressed tin, upholstered plywood, or beaded board can be used instead of corrugated metal.

It's distressing when historic buildings loaded with character are destroyed, so we try to salvage what we can. Lovely mantels are among the most likely junk candidates for search and rescue.

Primitive wood pieces and comfortable upholstered furniture evoke the feeling of welcome in this cottage living room. Reading material is handily displayed on a rack made from crib rails, a piece of baseboard, and carved corner blocks.

To create a cottage living room that is comfortable and inviting, follow a few basic guidelines. Keep it simple, fresh, open, and free from clutter. Primitive hutches and tables wearing chipped paint are must-haves if true cottage is your objective. Also, keep your paint colors fresh and your woodwork white. Junkables that suit the style include unexpected textures, such as a wire laundry basket employed as a table; the open-worked wire offers a pleasing departure from the heavier wood furnishings. Stick to basics and you will find yourself in a room you'll never want to leave. Piggy, the pooch, certainly seems content!

The dirty laundry will have to find a new home because this wire laundry basket is now occupied as a side table. All you need to do is add a piece of glass. No fuss, no muss. This is a project anyone can tackle.

Ornate metal bases pair up with plant stand pieces to form romantic pedestal candleholders. Do you like them? Say I do to this proposal.

85

{Simple Dining Done Well}

Give your cottage dining room a facelift by including a few soft-spoken pieces of junk. When simplicity is your objective, opt for clean lines and you'll be right on target!

W hen it's dinnertime at your cottage, make simplicity the house special. The minimalist approach is a good decorating strategy for an updated cottage dining room. To keep the look from being too austere, add warmth with inconspicuous junk. For example, to make a simple but unusual centerpiece, combine old bedsprings with artichokes and candle cups. Look for bedsprings at city or neighborhood cleanups and take one home for free! Check floral supply shops and crafts stores for candle cups on pointed stems; they're made for turning any vegetable or fruit into a candleholder. Quirky cabinets are standard cottage fare. Here a cabinet made from an outdated radiator cover found at a building reuse center stores serving vessels. What more could you wish for in a dining room? Well, maybe some pot roast with potatoes and carrots would be nice!

Snip individual bedsprings and wrap each coil around an artichoke to make creative candleholders.

Limited storage seems to be a universal problem. Consider this solution. Remove the front metal screen from an old radiator cover. Build shelves and incorporate the metal screen as lips on the shelves.

{Sun-Drenched Porch}

Style a space with junk and create a room that has a sunny disposition. What could be better than lounging on a cozy cottage porch quietly taking in the beautiful outdoors?

To capture the heart of cottage decor, stick to beaded board ceilings, painted wood floors, rugs made from natural fibers, and traditional white Adirondack furnishings. Flowers and plants add an element of nature that's essential to decorating an open-air space. Display them in a birdcage repurposed as a planter (for instructions, see page 94). If you have (or find) a child-size Adirondack chair, turn it into a table: Place a purchased round glass top on the arms or, if the arms slant backward, cut blocks of wood that will hold the glass in a level position (see page 90). The seat is a good place to stash extra magazines or books for summer reading.

Post travel plans or vacation pictures on a bulletin board made from an old screen door (see page 92 for how-to instructions). This handy notice board is too big for most kitchens, but it would work well in a teen's room, an office, or a shared study area to keep homework, invitations, recent photos, and upcoming events in plain sight.

To raise the tabletop to the perfect height for the chairs, rest the glass on blocks of wood. Keep the glass from slipping by sandwiching clear rubber stops or surface protectors (available from hardware stores) between the glass and the wood.

Pair fence pickets and abandoned window screens to create a shoe shelf large enough for the whole family (plus a neighbor kid or two).

The bird is missing, and the cat has a guilty look in its eyes. OK, so now what do you do with the vacated cage? Turn it into a planter! (See page 94 for instructions.)

Bulletin Board

MATERIALS NEEDED

screen door
plywood
screws
corkboard
construction adhesive
hinges
wall hangers

TOOL LIST

drill
saw
tape measure
screwdriver
jigsaw or utility knife

Bulletin Board Assembly

Step 1 Remove the screen, any trimwork, nails, and hinges from the door.

Step 2 Cut off the bottom half of the door.

Step 3 Cut the plywood to size and attach it to the back of the door with screws.

Step 4 With a jigsaw or utility knife, cut the cork to fit the openings and glue the cork pieces to the plywood with construction adhesive.

Step 5 For a shelf, attach the board from the bottom of the original door to the bottom of the bulletin board, using the original hinges and screws.

Step 6 Screw wall hangers on the back.

Many worn-out screen doors end up on the burn pile, but not if we can help it. They hold a ton of potential for junk-style decor. For example, instead of cork, this old door could frame mirror or recycled chalkboard slate.

Birdcage Planter

MATERIALS NEEDED

birdcage
chain
4 S hooks
cocoa matting
sheet moss
spring or clip
stand

TOOL LIST

wire or bolt cutter
utility knife

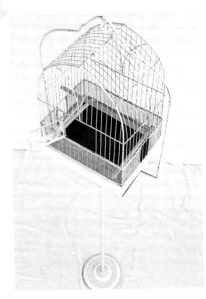

Planter Assembly

Step 1 Remove the bottom tray, feeding dishes, and perches.

Step 2 With wire cutter, cut off the bottom third of the cage.

Step 3 Turn the cage upside down. Cut four lengths of chain to reach from the corners to the desired height above the center of the cage (see photo *opposite*). Use S hooks to attach chains to corners.

Step 4 Line the cage with cocoa matting. From the outside, press sheet moss between the cocoa matting and the wires.

Step 5 Connect the chains with a spring or other connector and hang from the hook at the top of the stand. Fill with soil and plants.

Note: Use a stand that is sturdy enough to support the weight of damp soil and plants.

Pet birds have upgraded their housing, leaving a lot of old birdcages on the market. We had to use the cages somehow—they're too darn cute to waste.

The Fun House

Fun House decorating is for the young-at-heart. All you need is self-confidence, the ability to laugh at yourself, and the willingness to set your inner child free. We think Peter Pan put it best: "I won't grow up, I won't grow up!" Sound familiar? Then the Fun House home is for you.

DRINK
Coca-Cola
IN BOTTLES
live
shine
true
blew
ANT FARM
MAD
LUNCH-BOX
THE LONE RANGER
SCOTT BRUCE
LUNCH BOX: THE FIFTIES AND SIXTIES

Y ou can't help smiling when you look at this grown-up playroom. It moves one step beyond typical design thriftiness to employ things you can get *really* cheap! Corral miscellaneous junk from flea markets, yard sales, and your own home to capture this look. You'll save money, and your creations will, without a doubt, be quirky. A lamp made from a candy displayer and colander, *below*, is a good example of a comical combination. Wire it with lamp parts purchased from a lighting store. Introduce mismatched pillows and fabrics and mix in some downright silly junk to shape your room into something spectacular. Tuck a glass jar inside a roller skate and pop in a colorful bouquet. Use a punching-bag stand as sculpture and a pogo stick hung from a wall-mounted mailbox as wall art. Choose things that make you laugh; then play with the arrangement until the room displays a sense of humor.

Clever presentation plays an important role in this decorating style. A ball holder, acquired from a 1960s gym teacher, becomes an unusual side table when you add a round glass top. A toy truck becomes a remote control caddy, and an old candy displayer is wired up as a lamp, with a colander for a shade.

Finding the traditional backpack too small to hold all her flea market finds, Sue opts for the spacious back basket.

99

Discarding a broken-down croquet set is a definite no-no in the junker's handbook. A junker's motto: When all else fails, make it a candleholder (see page 102 for instructions).

Here's another campy art idea. Adorn your wall with a golden swordfish. If you can't find one made from pure 24 karat, use a can of gold spray paint.

sh ine

Attach phonetic word drill cards to a snack bag displayer and practice up on all the new words your children have learned at school! Or post a succinct message, such as "Clean up your room."

Newspapers are a necessary evil. You can't live with them; you can't find out about all the good estate sales without them. Here's a way to store those unsightly want ads: Wheel in a used paint striper (for applying those yellow lines on the road) and load it up. Behind it, an electrical box (used to store electricians' tools at a work site) stands in as a side table.

101

Croquet Candleholder

MATERIALS NEEDED

croquet stand or scrap wood
croquet balls
construction toys
wood glue
screws

TOOL LIST

pry bar, if needed
saw
tape measure
pencil
drill
Forstner bit, to match candle
   diameter (shown with
   $^7/_8$" bit)
screwdriver

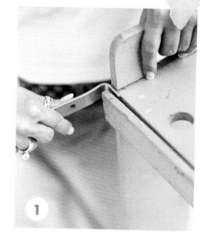

Candleholder Assembly

Step 1 Pry apart croquet stand to use one side for the base or use scrap wood (base shown is 5"×26").

Step 2 Drill into the top of the ball using the Forstner bit. Make the hole deep enough to hold the candle. Practice on a scrap block of wood to ensure a good fit.

Step 3 Measure and mark equal distances for the balls on the bottom of the base.

Step 4 Attach construction toy wheels to the bottom of the base, using glue and screws (drill off-center to avoid hitting the dowel).

Step 5 Working from the bottom, drive a long screw through the base at each mark. Predrill the bottom of each ball; screw the ball onto the protruding screw tip.

Note: Predrill screw holes to keep wood from splitting.

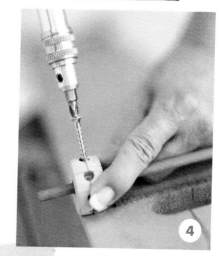

Reviving a piece of junk that is seemingly beyond repair gives us great satisfaction. Making it functional as well is a junker's dream come true. Take the challenge and see how clever you can be!

{ Wacky Workstation }

li ve

sh ine

tr ue

blew

Carve out a workspace in a corner of the family room, using a rug and wall-mounted shelves to define the area.

104

Who said that paying bills has to be a gloomy chore? Put yourself in a Fun House office and see how it improves your mood. Use a fail-safe formula when decorating in this style: Pick out a few essential pieces of functional furniture—a clean-lined desk and a retro modern chair. Then turn on the fun meter and assemble some quirky accessories. Post reminders and snapshots on a magnet board made from bowling pins and old metal signage numbers (see page 108 for how-to). Keep extra pencils in a barber's jar and stash stationery in a bread box. Instead of the usual filing cabinet, store papers and notebooks in a bright red tool chest. Now that you have a great place to work, wouldn't it be nice if you had leftover cash after paying the bills? One can always dream!

Think ice cube trays are obsolete? Think again. This one houses colored pencils. These trays can also hold earrings, paper clips, beads, or loose change.

Life is complicated; projects don't have to be. Instantly create a pencil holder out of a barbershop jar originally used to hold a solution for cleaning combs. Now, where will you store that collection of black plastic combs?

Ki inspects an ice cube tray for junk-worthiness.

105

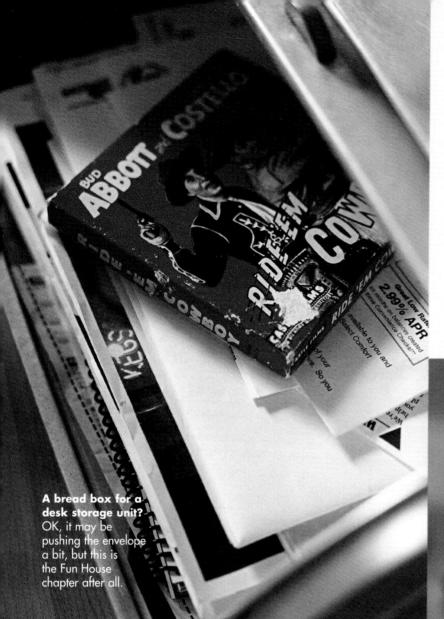

A bread box for a desk storage unit? OK, it may be pushing the envelope a bit, but this is the Fun House chapter after all.

Use this to keep bread in? Weird. I never would have thought of that.

Frame your favorite photo in a vintage restaurant napkin holder. If you collect molded plastic toys, they'll fit right in with Fun House decorating.

Spend some time with your junk collection and you'll be amazed by the creative ideas that will start popping into your head.

Organize photos, stamps, and other personal items on your desk with this bowling pin magnet board. Take a closer look at the desk and you'll spot an old 45-rpm record holder employed as a mail sorter (plus Olive Oyl standing at attention to guard all your important documents).

Make an incomplete set of dominoes into magnets. Purchase heavy-duty magnetic strips at your local hardware store and adhere to one side of the domino. It's as simple as that.

Bowling Pin Magnet Board

MATERIALS NEEDED

wood for base and top

2 bowling pins

2 metal numbers
   (test to see if magnets
   will stick to them)

wood trim (optional)

finishing nails and glue

screws

clear silicone

peel-and-stick magnets

dominoes

wood putty, to fill
   holes in bottoms
   of pins if necessary

TOOL LIST

saw

tape measure

router with V groove bit

hammer

drill

screwdriver

Magnet Board Assembly

Step 1 Cut wood base and top to fit pins and numbers (shown 7"×18").

Step 2 Adjust the project to work with the numbers and pins you have. We've added an additional smaller base (shown 3"×16") to raise the pins so the numbers fit.

Step 3 Rout a groove centered on the underside of the top piece (to hold the tops of both numbers). Rout two grooves centered horizontally on the sides of the base (to hold the bottoms of the numbers).

Step 4 Cut trim and attach to the base and top with glue and finishing nails.

Step 5 Use long (2") screws to attach pins to the base, working from the bottom of the base.

Step 6 Apply a small amount of clear silicone in the grooves; set the numbers into the grooves.

Step 7 Attach the top to the pins with 2" screws.

Step 8 Attach magnets to dominoes (use strong magnets that will hold business cards, etc.).

Note: Predrill screw holes to prevent wood from splitting.

Bowling pins can be found by the hundreds at flea markets. Ideas for how to use them are more scarce. This project is categorically crazy, but lives up to Fun House style requirements.

Apparently, Elvis is alive, well, and presiding over this kitchen. It seems fitting, considering his reputation for enjoying his food. Under The King's supervision, this room balances rock-'n'-roll excess with the order that every good kitchen needs. To match this look in your own kitchen, consider a tactic we call clutter control. Some collectors (you know who you are) display all their treasures simultaneously, and the room can quickly shift from menagerie to mind-boggling mess. Under the clutter control plan, you store some of your goodies away and then rotate the stored stuff into the display every so often. You'll find that after you haven't seen a possession for a month or two, it has as much impact as a newly purchased item. Once clutter is under control, a kitchen will come together in a snap. Here the eccentric decor—lunch boxes, lime green table, mix-and-match chairs, and colorful pottery—is an ideal backdrop for fanciful projects. A child's toy for a paper towel holder? Sure. A dartboard lazy Susan? Why not? It rocks! Stack those hip anodized aluminum drinking glasses in a wire rack store fixture (they're tucked between the clock and the mixer). Mr. Presley would approve.

How could they cover up that beautiful 1978 harvest gold refrigerator with stickers? It went so well with the 1976 avocado green stove!

Peanut butter and honey on white bread—yum! Like a dartboard lazy Susan, it's practical and fun at the same time. To make your own turntable, mount a dartboard on a swivel mechanism purchased at a woodworking store (see page 114 for instructions).

Junking Tip

Garage, tag, and moving sales offer some of the same items found at flea markets—and typically at a better price.

If you're looking for kitschy junk such as kids' toys, these venues are good options. Plan to arrive early on the first day of the sale; you'll get the best selection. If something is out of your price range, go back later to see if **the price has come down.**

A Jig Saw Jr. doubles as a paper towel holder (see page 110 for another view). Remove the blade and bend the bar to hold toweling securely.

A grid of open shelves cries out for a collection. What's a good choice for a Fun House home? Lunch boxes—and lots of them. Collecting lunch boxes can be surprisingly expensive, however, so slip in a few reproductions to save on cost. Like designer jeans paired with a discount store T-shirt, the mix of high- and low-end expresses your own sense of style.

When your child outgrows training wheels, hang them in your kitchen as dish towel hooks. They also work well as hooks in a child's playroom or bathroom. (Training pants we deem unfit for repurposing; dispose of them as you wish.)

Sure, she looks silly now, but wait until you see her pop a wheelie.

113

Dartboard Lazy Susan

MATERIALS NEEDED

scrap wood

lazy Susan swivel
(found in local hardware
or woodworker's store)

screws

dartboard

clear rubber stops or
surface protectors (from
a hardware store)

round glass cut to fit dartboard

TOOL LIST

tape measure

saw

drill

screwdriver

Lazy Susan Assembly

Step 1 Cut a wood base to fit the lazy Susan swivel mechanism.

Step 2 Attach the swivel mechanism to the wood with screws.

Step 3 Center the swivel mechanism on the underside of the dartboard and attach with screws.

Step 4 Press surface protectors onto the dartboard.

Step 5 Place precut round glass on the surface protectors.

Note: Always predrill screw holes to prevent wood from splitting.

114

Lazy Susans are making a comeback! If dartboards don't work with your color scheme, choose another round, flat piece of junk or even a slice of a tree to make your own spinning server.

Upbeat, lively, yet tasteful is the design directive for Fun House design. Inspiration for this bedroom came from the vintage advertisement for carrots, *right,* and a completely unrelated—but strikingly colorful and unusual—gear mold. To use a gear mold as a headboard, simply bolt it to the wall and slide your mattress and frame into position in front of it. Notice the bed linens—a lucky find featuring an abstract design that recalls gears. For storage, stack cases beside the bed; the ones pictured here once held roller skates, but old suitcases or doll trunks would work too.

Here's Ki, changing the hubcap on her monster truck.

To make this funky floor lamp, combine an old metal stool, lamp-wiring parts, and pipe purchased at a home improvement store. No sleeping in—it's up 'n' atom time.

117

When on the road, you have to take advantage of comfort where you find it.

Quirky and colorful, this tidy stack of roller skate cases makes a fabulous bedside table. Use the lower cases to store out-of-season clothing. The top one is convenient enough to hold in-season items.

Old table legs just keep on walking—or in this case, hanging. A table leg coatrack is the perfect solution in a room with limited storage (see page 120 for instructions).

Junking Tip

When shopping at a flea market, start with the outdoor vendors first. Inside the buildings you're likely to find more fine antiques, but outside is where the junk is! Look beyond the tabletops; hunt for boxes stashed under the tables to find the real bargains. Vendors often will have boxes of stray parts such as mismatched table legs. You can buy one leg or the whole box.

If you take the whole box, you're likely to get a better deal.

Table Leg Coatrack

MATERIALS NEEDED

door header (shown 42")
assorted table or chair legs
wood glue
screws

TOOL LIST

tape measure
pencil
miter box
saw
drill
screwdriver

Coatrack Assembly

Step 1 Measure and mark placement for legs.

Step 2 Using the miter box, cut the fat ends of the legs at an angle (shown cut at a 23-degree angle, 7" long).

Step 3 Apply glue to the angled ends of the legs and attach the legs to the header from the back. Use two screws per leg, if possible, to keep the legs from spinning.

Step 4 Use screws to attach the header directly to the wall.

Note: Always predrill screw holes to prevent wood from splitting.

If a table is no longer sturdy enough for its original purpose, salvage its parts. Table legs are handy pieces to have in your junk closet, ready for use in future projects.

Redefined Country

The natural comfort of country design combines with a dash of sleek, a pinch of urban, and a smidgen of humor to create redefined country. Leave the clutter behind and venture into new territory: nontraditional country decorating. Your rooms will feel light, airy, and altogether refreshing, like a farmhouse porch on a spring morning.

123

A backdrop of white combined with faded shades of blue and green creates a new country attitude: upbeat, modern, and crisp, yet still cozy.

Turn your bathroom into a country spa, a place where you can relax, unwind, and reflect. How do you create such an environment? Surround a claw-foot bathtub, a standard of traditional country design, with projects and ideas that have a more contemporary or industrial feel. Note the blending of different textures and styles here: The steel caddy is modern, the metal stool is more industrial, and the towel rack adds a hint of homespun creativity. The result is a room that sings in perfect three-part harmony.

A vase of flowers lifts the mood in any room. The fragrance will elevate your country bathroom to a country spa.

When your muscles are weary from the daily grind, relax in a candlelit bathtub. Fashion a wall-mounted candle display by hanging vintage shaving mirrors on an old door panel. Secure the door panel to wall studs and attach the mirror stands with hardware. Use a level to position both the panel and the mirrors and secure the mirror edge to the wood door with a waterproof, extra-strength glue.

Turn an outdated playpen into a rolling towel rack
(see page 128 for how-to).

Abandoned refrigerator drawers make excellent bathroom storage. You'll need the help of a welder to build a metal frame that accommodates your assortment of drawers. The result is a tower that contains all your bathroom odds and ends. Your next project? Building kitchen cabinets out of cotton swabs and toilet paper.

Gather up all those bathroom necessities that you'd rather not have on public display and tuck them away in a vintage waxed paper holder. Hang it on the wall, close the door, and stand back to admire your handiwork.

If you're looking for inexpensive shelving, look no further. Toilet tank lids mounted with metal L brackets and toggle bolts are an innovative and cost-conscious solution. Pick up some at your local building reuse center and put a lid on your shelving dilemma.

Playpen Towel Rack

MATERIALS NEEDED

- playpen
- bolts
- nuts
- screws
- casters

TOOL LIST

- saw
- tape measure
- drill
- screwdriver
- pliers

Towel Rack Assembly

Step 1 Cut down the two folding sides of the playpen to desired length for base and top (shown with a finished base size of 19").

Step 2 Reattach the base with nuts and bolts. Cut the top pieces at an angle (see photo *opposite*) and assemble with nuts and bolts.

Step 3 Using screws, attach leftover rails as support crossbars to stabilize the rack.

Step 4 Attach casters with screws.

Note: Always predrill screw holes to prevent the wood from splitting.

Baby's loss is our gain. The spacing of the rails on this old playpen is perfect for hanging towels. Sometimes in the junking world you just get lucky!

Bold red cabinets, textured walls, and granite countertops feel right at home in an updated farm kitchen.

old colors, stainless steel, and straight lines contribute
to a clean, pared-down country look. Notice anything
missing? Clutter has flown the coop. Your mission is to
maintain an orderly decor, so enhance your countertops
with junking projects that please the eye and help the
kitchen function well. You'll love the outcome: a kitchen
without chaos!

Stamp out disorder
with this clever concept,
left. Keep your everyday
spices close at hand
by suspending the
bottles in a rescued
rubber stamp holder.

With its cheese-cutting
days long past, this utensil
takes on the role of soap
holder, *above.*

131

Islands take center stage in kitchen redos. In a redefined country kitchen, metal stools with worn wood seats complement conventional country beaded board. The container full of vegetables is a retired electric casserole.

Red-handled potato mashers fitted with alligator clips make clever recipe holders. Use a small screw to attach the clip to the wooden handle; look for the clips at electronics stores or in the automotive section of hardware stores.

• Title Mahi Mahi w/ grilled Julienne [V]____
• Serves 4
• Favorite recipe from Kris
• Ingredients _____

- 4-(6-7) ounce Mahi Mahi Filet
- 1 tablespoon fresh minced gar[lic]
- 1 tablespoon fresh minced g[inger]
- 1 tablespoon extra virgin oli[ve oil]
- pinch of salt and pepper
- vegetables of choice

• Method _____

Prepare Mahi Mahi, season the [fish] with salt & pepper. Combine the [?] olive oil ginger and garlic and rub evenly over Mahi. Place f[ish] on a preheated cleaned grill. [grill] should be very hot.

Prepare julienne vegetables [?] [in] a large saute pan over medium flame. Add vegetables to oil gin[ger] & garlic.

• Notes _____
         Yummy!

Sue "The Masher" Whitney shopping for some of her signature accessories.

133

Ki punches out for a lunch break; then it's back to the junk assembly line.

Three little lunch boxes all in a row—plant them with herbs and watch them grow. To protect the lunch boxes and to keep the soil from becoming waterlogged, line the boxes with plastic saucers and transfer the herbs to plastic pots with drainage holes.

Sometimes when you find interesting junk, you haven't the foggiest notion of its intended purpose, *above right*. We used this unidentified rusty junk (URJ) to keep the napkins in their place.

Every family needs a little spot in the kitchen where they can sit down for a cup of coffee or a quick lunch, *opposite*. Buy an inexpensive 36-inch round glass top and perch it on an inventive base. Any guesses on the origin of this base? Would you believe vintage wheelchair wheels? Find a welder to craft a steel pedestal and connect the wheels to it.

Modern country means fun. Mix standard country fare with unconventional pieces, such as the wheelchair table, for a warm and lively look.

Keep your back entry organized
and tidy with a storage unit made
from old-fashioned mailboxes.

7253   6130   6128

6040   6034   6135

7263   7241   7255

Simply remove your sneakers, slip them in the mailbox, close the door, and poof, they're out of sight. Tuck a charcoal pad inside each mailbox to minimize unpleasant odors.

Junking Tip

Building reuse centers are excellent junking territory; check the Yellow Pages or the Internet for one in your neck of the woods. These stores have nearly everything a junker could want, including the kitchen sink. If you don't find what you want the first time, keep checking back. New junk is often brought in on a daily basis.

Entryways can be a storage nightmare. Shoes, hats, gloves, and other miscellaneous articles combine to create an unsightly mess. What to do? Here's a suggestion: Make a tidy stack of mailboxes capped with a wood top (see page 138 for instructions). Take it one step further and assign a mailbox number to each member of the family. This way you'll always know which box gets the stilettos and which box gets the sneakers.

Mailbox Shoe Rack

MATERIALS NEEDED

9 mailboxes
washers, nuts, and bolts
2×4 boards
casters
1×4 boards
wood trim
paint

TOOL LIST

drill
metal drill bit
tape measure
pencil
saw
paintbrush

Shoe Rack Assembly

Step 1 Drill a hole in the center of each long side of the mailboxes.

Step 2 Using washers and nuts, bolt three boxes together horizontally. Repeat with remaining boxes to create three sections of three boxes each.

Step 3 To raise the top row of boxes so the doors on the middle row can open, cut twelve 4"-long blocks from 2×4s. Drill a center hole in each.

Step 4 Drill two holes in the bottom of each top-row box to line up with the holes in the wood blocks. Drill matching holes in the top of each middle-row box. Also drill holes in tops and bottoms of mailboxes to connect middle and bottom rows.

Step 5 Attach horizontal sections with nuts and bolts, inserting 2×4 blocks between rows. Using nuts and bolts, attach casters to the bottom section.

Step 6 From 1×4s and trim, make top to fit. Paint or finish as desired.

We get excited about some pretty weird things, and these mailboxes were no exception. Fanatical about organization, we knew these black beauties could be put to work in our clutter containment program.

amily assemblies often revolve around numbers. (How many people are coming? How old are you today? How many years have we been married?) So why not use numbers as a decorating theme? Numbers add a nice graphic element that you wouldn't normally find in the classic country dining room. Integrate digits of all different shapes and sizes into place settings, wall art, and displays. Invite mismatched chairs to the table to create the relaxed look that characterizes country dining. Add a colorful table runner fashioned from old awning fabric. Now all the space lacks is one big happy family, two dogs, and eight plates of delicious home-style cooking.

Here's a happy find and a creative marriage, *right and opposite*: Adorable little three-legged casters have a rimmed opening that's the perfect size for a glass lampshade. Pop in a votive and you have light to go.

Tell your guests to take a number. Old house numbers are an easy way to assign seating. They may also help you take a head count at the end of a wild dinner party.

Recycled slate from a one-room schoolhouse and an interesting machine part come together as a menu board. The board could also post messages in the kitchen or entry hall.

Serve up farm-fresh dessert in style. Clamp a cake plate to a green metal skate sharpening vise to create a server with a bit of sass. Call this combination "black tie and sneakers."

Set the hutch for a help-yourself coffee and dessert buffet. The metal picnic baskets on top of the hutch are more than mere decoration: They stow seasonal entertaining supplies. For a country-themed accent, plant a miniature field in a watertight toolbox. Pat wheat berries (from a health food store) into clean potting soil and keep the soil moist. Once the grass sprouts, move the toolbox into sunlight so the grass will grow. Dress up the hutch with your kids' artwork for another playful element.

Built-in shelves provide the perfect opportunity to show off your collection of numbers or another collection of your choice. Add a few fresh country flowers, and before you can count to three, your shelves will come to life, providing a colorful backdrop for family and friends. Laughter is good for the soul. Incorporate little touches that amuse you. Here is an inside piece of information that's sure to make you smile: The numbers displayed on this built-in cost less than $5!

Sue practices for the Junk Olympics. Her sport? Rhythmic Junking.

A picket fence hanging bed is not too hard, not too soft, but just right for a long summer's nap. To make this comfy bed, attach short, well-worn pickets to an iron bed frame and suspend it from the ceiling with rusty chain and heavy-duty eye hooks. If you decide to make one of these, beware: The neighbors may be swinging by a little too often.

Leave the bustling sounds of the city behind and experience a new level of relaxation. Turn a summer kitchen into a sleeping porch to create your own private sanctuary. Start with a spectacular project and go from there. This peaceful environment boasts a swinging bed as the main attraction. Use heavy-duty hooks to attach the chains to the bedsprings and rest a mattress on top. For a bedside table, visit restaurant supply shops to look for a folding stand and large serving tray. Go ahead, treat yourself!

Three bad chairs can make one fabulous bench. Incorporate everything except the chair seats (save them for another project). Are some of your chairs missing legs? No problem. Borrow some from other chairs. Mix, match, and make it up as you go along (see page 148 for instructions).

A shabby sawhorse and a bikeless basket pair up as a three-season porch magazine rack. It's a cute little pack animal that requires little care.

Restaurant supply stores that carry used items are an excellent resource for battered metal trays. Although too worn for restaurant use, the trays are perfect as tabletops. Attach with screws to the top of a tray stand and you'll have a fine table that's not likely to be damaged by ever-changing weather.

Who needs to do dishes when so many clean ones are available?

"IN THE PAGES OF GOOD BOOKS
LIES THE MAGIC TO INSPIRE OUR
DREAMS AND THE POWER TO MAKE
THOSE DREAMS COME TRUE".

Keep your writing supplies or other small items tucked away in boxes made from frayed books (see page 150 for how-to). Stack the book boxes on top of each other for a charming display (guests will assume you're very well-read).

An industrial tool cabinet serves as a storage unit on the porch. It's a simple and attractive way to keep your extra blankets nearby for those breezy summer nights.

147

Three-Chair Bench

MATERIALS NEEDED

2×4 boards
1×4 boards
screws
paint
3 old chair backs with legs
4 assorted chair legs

TOOL LIST

hammer
nails
tape measure
saw
screwdriver
paintbrush

Bench Assembly

Step 1 From 2×4s build a seat frame with crossbars. Make the frame long enough to span the chair backs (shown 52"×16").

Step 2 Cut 1×4s so they are 2" longer than the frame (for 1" overhang at each end). Attach with countersunk screws to the top of the frame, leaving ⅛" between the boards and a 1" overhang on the front (enough to cover the legs).

Step 3 Paint or finish the seat as desired.

Step 4 Attach the chair backs to the back of the seat frame with screws.

Step 5 Attach assorted legs to the front of the frame, using two screws in each leg. This will prevent the legs from twisting.

Note: Always predrill screw holes to prevent the wood from splitting.

Who would have thought miscellaneous chair parts could be so useful? Go check the garage, the alley, and the attic for more!

Book Box

old book
salvaged wood
wood glue
nails
screws
decorative hardware
    (optional)

TOOL LIST

utility knife
tape measure
saw
miter box
hammer
drill
screwdriver

Box Assembly

Step 1 Remove pages with a utility knife.

Step 2 Cut wood so it equals the width of the book's spine. Cut into four strips and miter the ends to build a frame that fits perfectly inside the cover.

Step 3 Glue and nail corners together.

Step 4 Glue the frame to the inside back cover and the spine. Secure with screws.

Step 5 Use glue and small screws to attach decorative hardware, if desired.

Note: Always predrill screw holes to prevent the wood from splitting.

Old books are easy to come by, especially ones in rough shape. Use them to make boxes. Save some of the illustrated pages and use them as inexpensive artwork.

Modern Mosaic

Classic contemporary style merged with hip junk makes a bold design statement. Funky junk includes just about anything from industrial has-beens to shiny used restaurant equipment. Assemble your own cool mix to create a modern mosaic.

A tanning bed, JunkMarket style!

This is an avant-garde approach to a classic contemporary dining experience. Roll in a gurney, remove the undesirable top, and replace it with a glass one. Voilà—a dining table. Spice up the space with accessory pieces that are equally distinctive. A mirrored bar, vintage barware, and glass block fruit containers go well with this updated look (see page 156 for how-to).

Impress your friends with your bartending knowledge. Whip up a champagne cocktail in no time with the help of your very own Bar Aid. Bartenders used to keep these on hand for cocktail emergencies.

The bar caddy is a tray rest from a restaurant supply store. It's topped with a simple chrome bathroom mirror. No need to attach the mirror; it is quite sturdy resting on the stand. All you have to do is stock it and invite friends over for a festive evening.

Glass Block Tray

MATERIALS NEEDED

glass block

wood chair legs
(may need to be cut
shorter; shown 2")

spray bottle filled with
equal parts antifreeze
and water*

screws

TOOL LIST

safety goggles

old chisel

hammer

drill

glass drill bit

screwdriver

*Note: Antifreeze is toxic.
Do not store the solution and
discard spray bottle.

Tray Assembly

Step 1 Wearing safety goggles, separate the glass block by gently tapping the chisel in the seam.

Step 2 Place the block halves on a flat surface. Using the glass drill bit, drill holes where the tray legs will be attached. Intermittently spray with the antifreeze solution to cool the bit and the glass.

Step 3 Gently screw the legs to the two glass block pieces (do not put pressure on the glass or it will crack).

Did you know that you can split a glass block in half? It happened to us quite by accident, but instead of broken dreams, we had a new junk idea.

This contemporary office illustrates the "less is more" design philosophy with its clean lines, neutral colors, and warm woods. Have fun mixing junk into your modern space, but avoid clutter at all costs. The sleek junk accoutrements subtly blend into the environment. On the desk is a toilet paper holder turned candy dish (we all need something sweet while paying bills) and a bar garnish container that now holds paper clips and other office supplies. The nifty trash can on the far side of the desk is definitely a novelty. In the 1950s it held umbrellas by the front door. Remember, say yes to junk and no to clutter.

Research and development are words to live by for all ardent junkers. To make inexpensive artwork like this, take black and white images with your camera and frame them with something surprising, such as tennis racket presses. The sleek styling and color of the wood are a perfect fit for this room (see page 162 for how-to instructions).

Warning: Junking can be passed genetically from one generation to the next.

This toilet paper holder was never used as originally intended, so go ahead and fill it with the sweets of your choice. When manufacturing companies shut down, they leave behind something called "new old stock"—manufactured items that were never used. You can find this type of product at flea markets and warehouse closeout sales.

Instead of cherries and olives, this bar condiment container neatly separates rubber bands, paper clips, and other office paraphernalia.

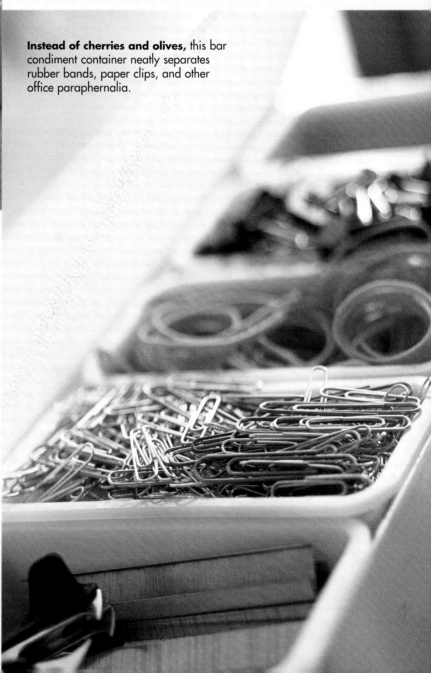

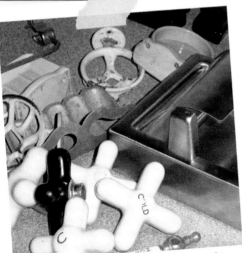

This toilet paper holder is destined to be a candy dish. Now that's what I call a Cinderella story!

160

The leader of this Mod Squad grouping is the side table fashioned from a rolling desk chair base. The original metal strips from the seat support the glass round. Use clear rubber surface protectors (from a hardware store) to keep glass in place. Bring in some groovy chairs from the '70s or '80s (sorry, folks, but the '80s are now considered vintage) and cross the finish line with a funky lamp.

This chair was stretched out and enjoying its retirement. We got it on its feet and put it back to work.

161

Racket Press Frame

MATERIALS NEEDED

tennis racket press

mat board

photo

tape

acrylic plastic
  (shown 1/16" thick)

wood finish

TOOL LIST

pencil

mat cutter or
  precision knife

straightedge/ruler

drill

glass drill bit

Frame Assembly

Step 1 Lay the racket press on the back of the mat board and trace around it.

Step 2 Using the mat cutter or precision knife and straightedge, cut two mats, being careful not to cut beyond the traced lines.

Step 3 Cut the photo opening in one mat (shown 4"×2"). Position photo in opening and tape it to wrong side of mat.

Step 4 Trace the racket press onto acrylic plastic. Using a precision knife and straightedge, score the acrylic plastic along the traced lines. Align the scored line with a table edge and snap off the excess plastic.

Step 5 Drill holes in the acrylic plastic to match the corners of the racket press, being careful not to apply too much pressure or get too close to the edge of the plastic. Drill matching holes through the mats.

Step 6 Finish the wood.

Step 7 Assemble the frame in this order: back of press, mat board backing, mat board with photo, acrylic plastic, front of press.

Note: To make this frame two-sided, add a second piece of acrylic plastic and cut a photo opening in both mats.

Consider all the angles when looking for framing options. We were motivated to make the presses into frames because their shape and color spoke a modern language that suits this style.

A glass block wall and shiny black granite countertops set the stage for a wine-tasting party à la junk. The icons of the event include stainless-steel warming lamps, industrial light covers, and an unusually shaped colander standing in as a fruit bowl. Now it's time to taste the vintage reds.

A sparkling contemporary kitchen of stainless steel, granite, and glass block may not seem like a good candidate for junk accoutrements, but look more closely: The recycled stuff blends so well that it's hard to tell what's junk and what's not. A vegetable storage unit on the counter beside the sink, a cookbook holder, metal wine bottle baskets, groovy candle containers, and unusual flower vases set this kitchen apart from ordinary ones. Summon your friends for an impromptu gathering and see if they can spot your hip junk.

Do these remind you of anything? Think middle school lunch line and go from there. These silverware containers from a cafeteria are the ultimate candleholders for a kitchen in pursuit of contemporary flair. What makes them contemporary? The cylindrical shape and geometric design are key ingredients.

Restaurant supply stores are a great resource for raw ingredients. Who knows what you'll cook up?

165

A metal sanitizer from a hospital serves as storage for potatoes and onions. Lock away the odor of the onions until you're ready to cook.

Medical office furnishings provide ample food for thought, inspiring a junker's wildest ideas. The cookbook holder is the inside of an ophthalmologist's cabinet. The light doesn't work, but it looks cool—and cool counts. If you want to make it operational, have it rewired by a professional or tackle it yourself if you're handy with wiring projects.

This is an ingenious idea. Sometimes you run across a piece and immediately recognize its purpose. In this case the industrial light covers said, "Make us wine bottle holders." Metal legs welded on the bottom keep them upright and wobble-proof.

Say yes to restaurant junk. What was once a warming lamp at a diner is now a vase. Remove the cord and flip the lamp upside down. The lamps aren't watertight, so insert plastic or glass containers to hold the flowers and water.

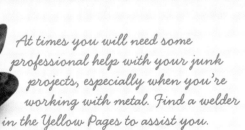

At times you will need some professional help with your junk projects, especially when you're working with metal. Find a welder in the Yellow Pages to assist you.

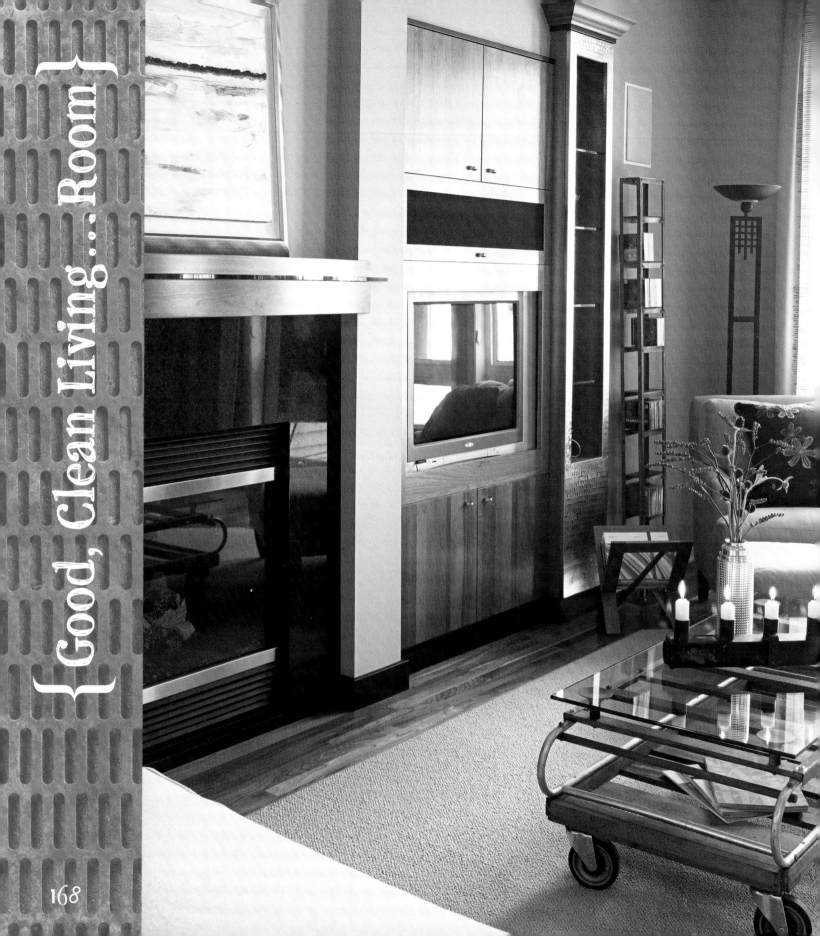

Here's a living room that is modern yet warm and inviting. The sleek metal-and-wood mantel and the metal display shelves set the contemporary tone. A few prominent pieces of junk handiwork introduce more personality. A metal tower of open shelves makes it easy to locate that CD you love. The table made from a car roof rack and an easel made from shuffleboard cues also make a modern statement. Keep tabletop adornments to a bare minimum. A shiny thermos flower vase and an industrial candleholder are sufficient.

Sue climbs the stairway to junk heaven.

Three shuffleboard cues make a fabulous easel for your most treasured art. Bolt the handles together at the top and use eyebolts and chain (attached to the cues about 18 inches from the floor) to hold the legs in the desired position. Attach an aluminum U bracket to support your artwork.

We found this piece at a building re-use center in the HVAC department. Having no idea what it was in its past life, we promptly removed the motor and electrical cord and filled it with candles.

Wow! This is one cool table. Removed from a 1957 station wagon, this hunk of junk, an old roof rack, has a new attitude and a new purpose. Connect the carrier to a wooden slatted base, using heavy metal screws (we used a leftover base from another project); add casters and a glass top. For your convenience, the carrier comes complete with suction cups to hold the glass top firmly in place.

A windmill ladder is reborn as a CD holder. Cut the ladder in half and put the halves together to make the front and back. Have a base and shelves welded to the frame.

You leave Sue alone with a
chain saw for 5 minutes and. . .

If you love logrolling, then this project is for you. Locate a tree removal company and ask them to cut tree trunks into 12-inch sections. Bring the sections home, attach casters, and you have benches that only nature can provide. By the way, they are sturdy enough for Paul Bunyan and Babe, his blue ox.

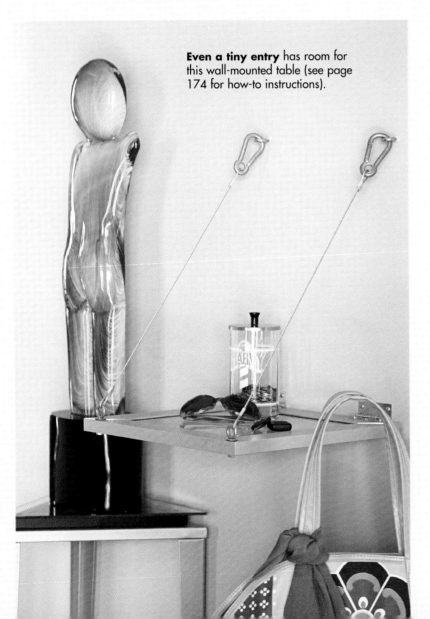

Even a tiny entry has room for this wall-mounted table (see page 174 for how-to instructions).

see page 174 for how-to instructions

Junking Tip

We've told you about many different places to junk, but we don't want you to miss out on this opportunity. A used office supply store is a true junk haven, particularly for contemporary junkers. You can find large pieces with great potential: old office partitions that could easily become an awesome headboard or room divider and sleek cabinets that can be taken apart and repurposed. You'll also find typical stuff such as desks and chairs, all at reasonable prices.

Change the way you look at contemporary decorating and take a more inventive approach. Junk adds an element that's totally unanticipated in a modern environment. Go ahead— shock the world and introduce contemporary junk!

173

Sleek Shelf

MATERIALS NEEDED

2 hinges

recycled cabinet door or window (shown 15" square)

screws

2 eyebolts, washers, and nuts

cable

cable clamps

2 clips

2 wall eye hooks

molly bolts (if necessary for your type of wall)

TOOL LIST

screwdriver

drill

pliers or wrench

tape measure

level

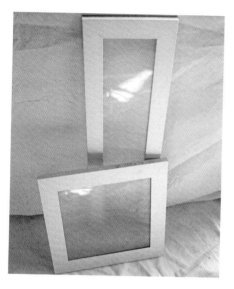

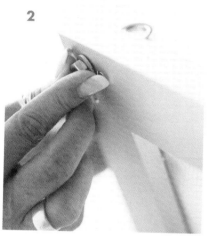

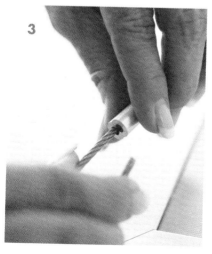

Shelf Assembly

Step 1 Attach hinges to the door with screws, making sure the pins extend just over the edge of the door (this allows the shelf to hang properly).

Step 2 Drill holes in the front corners of the shelf and push eyebolts through the holes (see photo *opposite* for placement). Secure the eyebolts with washers and nuts, tightening with pliers or a wrench.

Step 3 Thread the cable through the eyebolts and secure with cable clamps (some hardware stores will do this for you). Measure the length of cable needed to reach the wall above the shelf (shown 20"). Thread the cable through the clips and secure with cable clamps; check that the cables are exactly the same length to ensure a level shelf.

Step 4 Attach the eye hooks to the wall at the desired height, using molly bolts if necessary.

Step 5 Attach the clips to the wall eye hooks, then screw the hinges to the wall, checking that the shelf stays level.

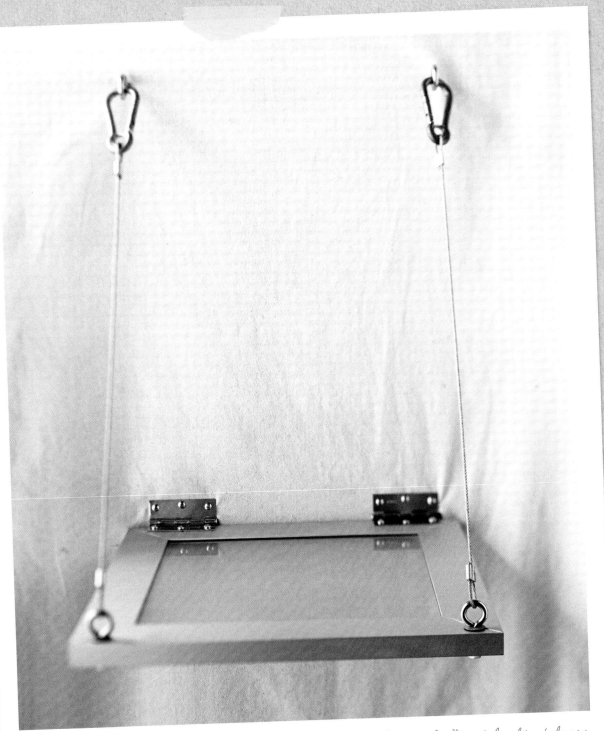

Castoffs pop up in different venues. We found some "irregular" metal cabinet doors at a building re-use center and had to have them. Paired with modern cables and clips, the once ordinary doors took on a cool new attitude.

Vintage Blend

Take all the design styles from the previous chapters, throw them in the blender, and flip the switch. The result? A perfect eclectic concoction we call Vintage Blend.

The junk transformation in this kitchen began with the center island, a counter from an old hardware store. If you find a similar piece, bring it back into action with a little tender loving care. Beware, however: You may have to clean out some animal droppings before taking your prize home. A paint job, industrial dolly parts for legs, and a snappy new top are major components for a store counter conversion. You may also have to reinforce some wood that has become too weathered over the years.

Offset old pieces with sleek contemporary additions. The revamped island is surrounded with stainless-steel appliances and modern light fixtures to establish an eclectic look.

If you're remodeling, consider custom-designing the countertop around a distinctive piece like this German washtub.

You know you're junking in Wisconsin when...

A cheese grater wired to a standard night-light filters the light for a soft glow—just enough to guide you to the sink for a glass of water.

This kitchen is no diner, so the barstools were dressed up. Before, they wore 1950s chrome and red leather. With a new finish over the chrome and a mix-and-match fabric makeover, they fit in nicely with the neorustic island.

This looks like a guillotine but serves a much more pleasant purpose. It's a cheese cutter that we put to use as a serving piece on the island.

After this photo was taken, the doctor stitched Ki's thumb right back on.

183

Oh but·ter·fly, say, Why will you

This writer's retreat is furnished almost entirely with reclaimed materials. Study the space carefully and you'll find a collection of mismatched furniture and accessories that combine to make a remarkable design statement. The wall-mounted bookshelf is made from heating-vent grates and an old ladder (see page 188 for how-to). What is the most inventive junkable in this room? Our vote goes to the wooden gear mold, which is suspended from a metal bracket to serve as a room divider (far left of photo). The fun part is that it actually spins! Writer's block? Certainly not in this room!

Making a table from a window has been done before, but the original casing and oval shape make this project more intriguing. Add table legs to complete the piece.

185

A wire basket gets legs from an old galvanized tub. Together they offer a practical way to store newspapers and magazines.

A well-ordered, inspirational writing space starts with a rescued table instead of a more traditional desk. Supply additional ambience with items such as an old-world globe, surveyor's equipment, and a reproduction telephone. Remember functional junk is best, especially in an office. The desk organizers include a canteen pen-and-pencil holder and a paper organizer made from the backside of a grate.

"Free!" It's the only four-letter word Sue can shout without having to put a dollar in the swear jar.

A junker's proverb: "In rust we trust." Almost every interesting piece of vintage metal has a little rust on it.

OOKNOTES

Stop! Don't throw leftovers away. After using the decorative front part of a grate for a project, you'll be left with the back regulator. Have legs welded into place and use it as a paper organizer.

187

Ladder Shelf

MATERIALS NEEDED

4 or 5 iron vents
   (shown 10"×12") to fit on
   rungs between side supports
old ladder
scrap wood blocks
wood finish
screws
threaded rod
8 flange connectors

TOOL LIST

saw and hacksaw
drill
tape measure
screwdriver

Shelf Assembly

Step 1 Remove regulator backs from vents.

Step 2 Saw the ladder to the desired height.

Step 3 Cut two wood blocks per vent (shown 3"×2"). Finish wood blocks and ladder as desired.

Step 4 Position a vent on a ladder rung. Using screws, attach the blocks to the inside of the ladder supports to secure vent. Fit should be snug. Repeat for remaining vents. Predrill holes to prevent the wood from splitting.

Step 5 Screw two flange connectors onto rod facing toward each other. Cut rod to the desired length (determined by vent depth, shown 3"). Repeat for remaining rods/flanges.

Step 6 With screws attach all flanges/rods to back of the ladder.

Step 7 Attach flanges/ladder to wall.

Grates are great finds. As multipurpose junk they make excellent bookshelves, interesting trivets, original wall art—you name it!

{ Dramatic Corridor }

PARQUET
SEATS 8 TO 18
E F
SEATS 1 TO 7
PARQUET
SEATS 1 TO 15
P Q
SEATS 11 TO 22
PARQUET
SEATS 8 TO 18
G H
SEATS 1 TO 7

An eclectic hallway boasts dramatic junk blended with contemporary materials such as metal and concrete. With a few minor adjustments, a ballet bar becomes a handrail on a staircase. Old theater lights illuminate black and white posters, casting a romantic glow over the space. The final touch is a junk-style shelf, pulling together a look that's bold and beautiful.

An obsolete car luggage rack finds new purpose as an entryway shelf support. What will you think of next?

Restored theater seating lights help pilot the way to the refrigerator for a midnight snack.

At last, we found it: the fabled Golden Table of Junklantis!

Step inside a Vintage Blend bedroom. Before you kick off your shoes, throw back the covers, and jump in bed for a much needed nap, look around to see how this room is put together. The appeal comes from the mix of textures and styles. To capture this look, incorporate metal, wicker, textiles, and wood and mix up elements of cottage, traditional, and vintage style with a dose of funky on the side. Aim to create a timeless design that exudes character and looks fresh and lovely at the same time.

Make the bed the focal point, *opposite and above right,* by hanging a shelf made from salvaged molding on the wall above. Keep the shelf display simple—a pair of photos and a plant—to minimize clutter.

An outdated hospital table removed from its typical sterile surroundings becomes an excellent bedside table, *below right.* Now all you have to do is find someone to serve breakfast.

Family and friends are neatly displayed for easy viewing on a revamped drying rack, *left.* Binder clips from an office supply store hold photos in place (see page 194 for how-to).

Drying Rack Photo Holder

MATERIALS NEEDED

wall-mount drying rack

about 8' of bead chain
(shown ⅛")

12 bead chain connectors

32 binder clips

32 screws (#6 shown)

32 washers

2 wall hangers

TOOL LIST

drill

wire cutter

tape measure

screwdriver

Photo Holder Assembly

Step 1 Predrill all the holes for the bead chain (drill bit size ⁵⁄₃₂").

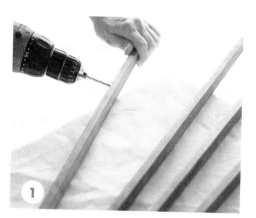

Step 2 Starting at the top row of holes, put a connector on one end of the chain and pull through the first hole. Cut the chain (ours was cut at 5"), put a connector on the cut end and thread through the next hole, and add another section of chain. Repeat to connect the remaining arms, ending with a connector. For the line of chain close to the base, use two connectors, one on each end, and string the chain through the holes without cutting.

Step 3 Predrill the screw holes for the binder clips. We started 3" down from the top, then every 6" down the length of each arm. Place the screw through the washer, then through the top of the clip.

Step 4 Attach two wall hangers on the back of the rack for hanging.

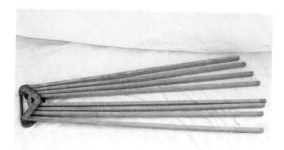

Drying racks are a bit passé yet still readily available, so dream up some fun projects for yourself. It gives us satisfaction to turn a mundane item like this into a work of art.

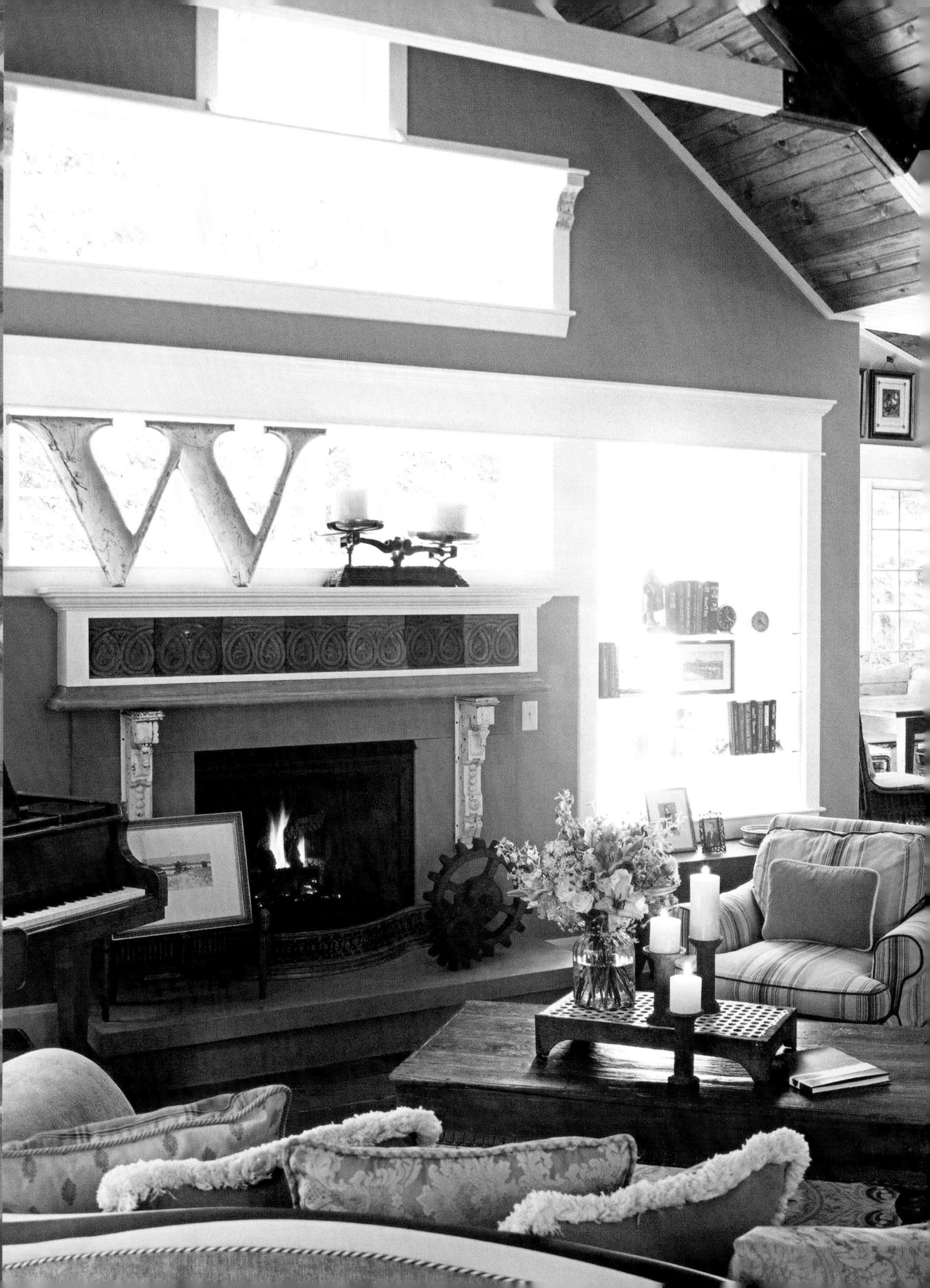

A glass top and metal base turn a wooden gear mold into a side table.

They can bench a combined weight of over 35 candleholders!

"OK, be honest: Does this gas heater go with my outfit?"

The W stands for wow! This great-looking room blends an assortment of ingredients: a wonderful sofa, traditional club chairs, an antique table, and exceptional junk accessories. It boasts comfort and style without overdoing a thing. If you are remodeling or building new, incorporate junk into the architecture of your home. For example, the fireplace here is made from concrete, recycled brick, and salvaged carved wood trim and corbels. The junk accoutrements include grates, candleholders made from disc spacers, and wood gear molds that stand in as sculpture. The artwork on the hearth rests on an outdated gas heater turned easel. The dark tones of worn wood and old metal harmonize with the wood plank ceiling and accent the crisp white woodwork and green walls.

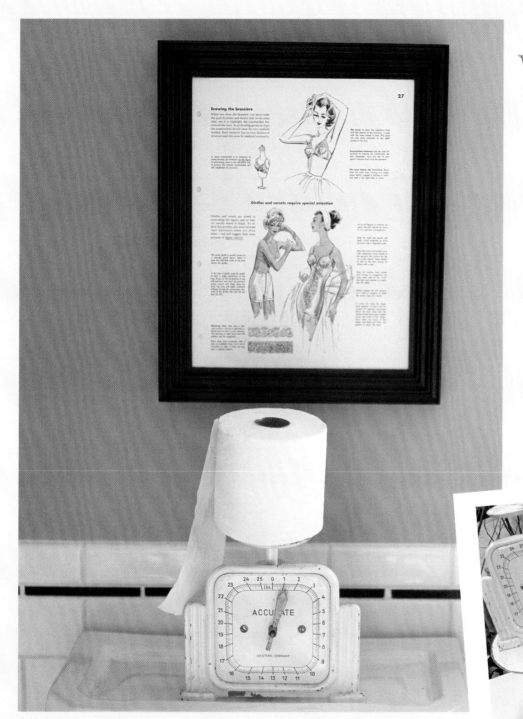

Vintage meets industrial in this bathroom. Hexagonal-tile floors reminiscent of chicken wire date to bungalows of the 1930s, and white brick-shape tiles say 1950s. Medicine cabinets made from old tin and a quaint chair with a rusty metal tray to hold bathing necessities also carry the vintage message. The industrial elements include the concrete countertop, exposed pipes, and metal storage cabinet (old safe-deposit boxes). The two styles make a dynamic duo.

Is this the Fun House chapter? No, but a little silliness belongs in every home. An advertising art book supplied this bathroom art. Everyone should learn to draw girdles and corsets properly, don't you think? Looks like the toilet paper needs to lose a few sheets!

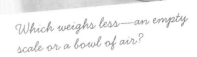

Which weighs less—an empty scale or a bowl of air?

What's behind door number 97? Congratulations! You've just won extra bathroom supplies neatly hidden away in a safe-deposit box.

"Rex is my name, towel holding's my game. I used to hold paper, but I like this gig better. The towels are much softer and not so heavy. I'm not getting any younger."

If you enjoy novel ideas, here's a good one: Old screen doors and windows were reassembled to make these shower doors and the transom window. They're set into the wall so you don't see the glass surround that encloses the shower.

Add romance to any room with a chandelier made from garden fencing (see page 202 for instructions). Above the bathtub it supplies soft candlelight. On a porch it could wear spring flowers instead of candles.

Wire Fence Chandelier

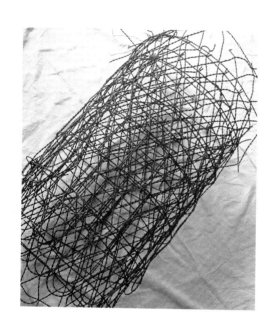

Chandelier Assembly

Step 1 Using a bolt cutter, cut a section of fence (shown 6' long × 18" high; note that fencing sizes vary). Leave wire tails to bend and connect the two ends.

Step 2 Connect the two ends of fence by twisting the wires together.

Step 3 Using the 18-gauge wire, attach the votive cups, jars, or insulators to the chandelier. Use the needle-nose pliers to twirl wire ends into spirals around the neck of each candleholder.

Step 4 Attach chains to hang.

This project is dear to our hearts because it was the first project created at the JunkMarket. It has now become our mascot and shows up in whatever we do—speaking engagements, television programs, and our sales. Please enjoy!

Index

Adirondack chairs, 88–90
Architectural salvage, 11
Artwork
    in bathroom, 199
    easel for, 169
    fireplace surround for, 10
    metal signage as, 34–35
    racket press frame, 159, 162–163
    scooters as, 44
    swordfish adornment, 100
    wall-mounted magazine rack, 45
Automotive salvage, 25

Bar caddy, 155
Bathrooms
    cottage-style, 78–79
    country spa, 124–127
    vintage, 198–201
Bedrooms
    European cottage, 12–13
    Fun House, 116–119
    tropical look for, 68–69
    urban loft, 30–31
    Vintage Blend, 192–193
Bedside table
    music stand as, 12–13
    roller skate cases as, 118
Bed tray, shutter, 69–71
Benches
    three-chair bench, 145, 148–149
    window wells for, 35, 38–39
Birdcage planter, 89, 91, 94–95
Books, old, 64, 147, 150–151
Bowling pin magnet board, 107–109
Bulletin board, 89, 92–93

Candle display, 124–125
Candleholders
    artichokes as, 86–87
    ashtrays as, 62–63
    camera lens as, 43
    croquet ball, 100,102–103
    glass lampshade, 52–53, 140–141
    industrial, 170
    mirror candle post, 31–33
    record player as, 45
    romantic pedestal, 85
    silverware containers as, 165
Candle platforms, 16–17
Candle tray, 19–21
CD tower, 168–169, 171
Chairs
    Adirondack, 88–90
    beauty parlor, 31
    as log holders, 9
    tables made from, 54–55, 161
    three-chair bench, 145, 148–149
Chandelier, wire fence, 201–203
Cheese graters, 24, 26–27, 181
Coatracks, 25, 119–121
Coffee tables
    junk garnishes on, 62–63
    from milk-bottling machine, 34–36
    from pipe and casters, 44–45
    from playpen, 8–9
Continental style
    defined, 7
    dining room, 16–17
    Euro bedroom, 12–13
    Italian kitchen, 22–25
    living room, 8–11
    solarium, 18–19

Cottage Collage
    bathroom, 78–79
    bedroom, 80–81
    defined, 73
    dining room, 86–87
    living room, 84–85
    porch, 88–89
    sitting room, 74–75
Country style, Redefined
    bathroom, 124–127
    description of, 123
    dining room, 140–143
    entry, 136–137
    kitchen, 130–135
    porch retreat, 144–147
Croquet candleholder, 100, 102–103

Desk accessory tray, 47–49, 160
Dining rooms
    continental-style, 16–17
    cottage-style, 86–87
    Redefined country style, 140–143
    modern, 154–155
    traditional, 52–53
    urban loft, 40–43
Drawer candle tray, 19–21
Drawer napkin holder, 53, 56–57
Drying rack photo holder, 193–195

Entryways
    contemporary junk for, 172–173
    redefined country look for, 136–137

Farm equipment, 19, 41
Farmhouses. See Redefined Country
Fun House design
    bedroom, 116–119
    croquet candleholder, 100,102–103
    defined, 96
    grown-up playroom, 98–101
    kitchen, 110–113
    workstation, 104–107

Glass block trays, 154–157
Grater shelves, 24, 26–27

Headboard
    bedsprings as, 30
    gear mold as, 116–117
    mantel as, 80–83
Home office. See Office space

Ice cube trays, 41, 105

Junking tips
    architectural salvage, 11
    building reuse centers, 137
    free stuff, 181
    kids' toys, 112
    office furniture, 173
    ordinary items, 55
    outdoor vendors, 119
    restaurant supply stores, 37

Kitchens
    farm kitchen, 130–135
    French Country, 60–61
    Fun House design for, 110–115
    Italian kitchen, 22–25
    modern kitchen, 164–167
    urban loft kitchen, 40–43
    Vintage Blend style for, 178–183
Knitting bag vase, 37

Ladder shelf, 188–189
Lamp
    beach umbrella as, 58
    camera tripod as, 34–35
    candy displayer as, 99
    stool as, 117

Lazy Susan dartboard, 111, 114–115
Living rooms
    continental, 8–11
    cottage-style, 84–85
    modern, 168–171
    traditional, 62–65
    urban loft, 34–37
    Vintage Blend, 196–197
Locker baskets, 47
Lunch boxes, 110, 112, 134–135

Magazine racks, 45, 65–67, 145, 186
Magnet board, bowling pin, 107–109
Mailbox shoe rack, 136–139
Mantel headboard, 80–83
Mirror candle post, 31–33
Mirrors, 9, 78–79, 125
Modern mosaic
    defined, 153
    dining room, 154–155
    entry, 172–173
    kitchen, 164–167
    living room, 168–171
    office, 158–161
Mop wringer, 24

Napkin holder
    drawer as, 53, 56–57
    as photo frame, 106

Office space
    Fun House, 104–107
    modern, 158–161
    urban loft, 46–47
    writer's retreat, 184–187

Paper organizer, 187
Paper towel holder, 23
Photo displayer
    carpenter's levels as, 54–55
    drying rack photo holder, 193–195
    napkin holder as, 106
    ruler easel as, 13–15
    shadow box, 69
Planter, birdcage, 89, 91, 94–95
Playpen
    coffee table from, 8–9
    screen cabinet from, 75
    towel rack from, 126, 128–129
Projects
    bed tray, 69–71
    benches, 35, 38–39, 145, 148–149
    birdcage planter, 89, 91, 94–95
    book box, 147, 150–151
    bowling pin magnet board, 107–109
    bulletin board, 89, 92–93
    chandelier, 201–203
    coatrack, 119–121
    croquet candleholder, 100, 102–103
    desk accessory tray, 47, 48–49
    drawer candle tray, 19, 20–21
    drawer napkin holder, 53, 56–57
    drying rack photo holder, 193–195
    framed vase, 74, 76–77
    glass block tray, 154–157
    grater shelves, 24, 26–27
    headboard, 80–83
    ladder shelf, 188–189
    Lazy Susan dartboard, 111, 114–115
    magazine rack, 65–67
    mailbox shoe rack, 136–139
    mirror candle post, 31–33
    racket press frame, 159, 162–163
    ruler easel, 13–15
    sleek shelf, 173, 174–175
    towel rack, 126, 128–129

Racket press frame, 159, 162–163
Restaurant supply stores, 37, 165
Ruler easel, 13, 14–15

Shelving
    ladder shelf, 188–189
    luggage rack as, 191
    sleek shelf, 173–175
    toilet tank lids as, 127
Shoe rack, mailbox, 136–139
Shoe shelf, 90–91
Shutter bed tray, 69–71
Suitcases, old, 30–31, 59
Sunporches, 88–89, 144–147
Sunrooms, 18–19, 58–59

Table leg coatrack, 119–121
Tables. See also Coffee tables
    from Adirondack chairs, 88–90
    from ball holders, 99
    from books, 64
    from car roof racks, 168–169, 171
    from church chairs, 54–55
    from dollies, 19
    from garden urns, 13
    from gurneys, 154–155
    from metal trays, 146
    from street lamps, 17
    from suitcases, 59
    from trash cans, 40, 43
    from wheelchair wheels, 134–135
    from window, 185
    from window washers, 45
    from wire baskets, 85
    from wooden gear molds, 197
Towel rack, playpen, 126, 128–129
Toys, 98–99, 106–107, 112
Traditional Twist style
    bedroom, 68–69
    defined, 51, 53
    dining room, 52–53
    kitchen, 60–61
    living room, 62–65
    photo displayers, 54–55
    sunroom, 58–59
Trays
    bed, 69–71
    desk accessory, 47–49
    drawer candle, 19, 20–21
    glass block, 154–157
    ice cube, 41, 105
    jewelry, 79
    Lazy Susan dartboard, 111, 114–115
    memo board, 17
    stool seat, 52–53

Urban loft decor
    bench project, 35, 38–39
    defined, 29
    dining area, 40–43
    living room, 34–37
    office space, 46–49
    retro rest area, 30–31
    wall art, 44–45

Vases
    framed vase, 74, 76–77
    knitting bags as, 37
    light fixtures as, 81
    restaurant lamps as, 167
    shiny thermos, 168–169
    watertight vessels, 11
Vintage Blend
    bathroom, 198–201
    bedroom, 192–193
    defined, 177
    hallway, 190–191
    kitchen, 178–183
    living room, 196–197
    writer's retreat, 184–187

Workstations. See Office space